The Scent of Time

Byung-Chul Han

The Scent of Time

A Philosophical Essay on the
Art of Lingering

Translated by Daniel Steuer

polity

First published in German as *Duft der Zeit. Ein philosophischer Essay zur Kunst des Verweilens* © transcript Verlag, Bielefeld, 2009

This translation is published by arrangement with transcript Verlag, Germany.

This English edition © Polity Press, 2017

Polity Press
65 Bridge Street
Cambridge CB2 1UR, UK

Polity Press
101 Station Landing, Suite 300,
Medford, MA 02155, USA

ISBN-13: 978-1-5095-1604-9
ISBN-13: 978-1-5095-1605-6 (pb)

A catalogue record for this book is available from the British Library.

Library of Congress Cataloging-in-Publication Data

Names: Han, Byung-Chul, author.
Title: The scent of time : a philosophical essay on the art of lingering / Byung-Chul Han.
Other titles: Duft der Zeit. English
Description: English edition. | Malden, MA : Polity, 2017. | Includes
   bibliographical references and index. |
Identifiers: LCCN 2017006857 (print) | LCCN 2017033663 (ebook) | ISBN
   9781509516070 (Mobi) | ISBN 9781509516087 (Epub) | ISBN 9781509516049
   (hardback) | ISBN 9781509516056 (pbk.)
Subjects: LCSH: Time. | Coincidence. | Time management. | Life. | Contemplation.
Classification: LCC BD638 (ebook) | LCC BD638 .H275713 2017 (print) | DDC
   115--dc23
LC record available at https://lccn.loc.gov/2017006857

Typeset in 10.75 on 14 Janson Text by
Servis Filmsetting Ltd, Stockport, Cheshire
Printed and bound in Great Britain by Clays Ltd, St. Ives PLC

For further information on Polity, visit our website:
politybooks.com

CONTENTS

PREFACE

Today's temporal crisis is not a crisis of acceleration. The age of acceleration is already over. What we experience today as acceleration is only *one* of the symptoms of temporal dispersal. Today's temporal crisis is caused by a dyschronicity which leads to various temporal disturbances and irritations. Time is lacking a rhythm that would provide order, and thus it falls out of step. Dyschronicity lets time whizz, so to speak. The feeling that life is accelerating is really the experience of a time that is whizzing without a direction.

Dyschronicity is not the result of a push for further acceleration. In the first place, it is the atomization of time which is responsible for dyschronicity. It is also the reason for the feeling that time passes much more quickly than it used to. Due to the temporal dispersal, no experience of duration is possible. Nothing *comports* time.[1] Life is no longer embedded in any ordering structures or coordinates that would found duration. Even things with which we identify are fleeting and ephemeral. Thus, we become radically transient ourselves.

The atomization of life goes hand in hand with an atomization of identity. All we have is our self, our little ego. We are subject to a radical loss of space and time, even of world, of being-with. Poverty of world is a phenomenon of dyschronicity. It reduces the human being to a tiny body that is kept *healthy* at all costs. Otherwise, what would we have? The health of one's fragile body is a substitute for world and God. Nothing outlasts death. Thus, dying is particularly difficult today. And we age, without becoming *old*.

This book investigates the causes and symptoms of dyschronicity in historical as well as systematic terms. But it also offers reflections on possibilities for recovery. While these touch upon heterochronic or uchronic moments, the present study is not limited to finding and rehabilitating these exceptional, extraordinary places of duration. Rather, its retrospection draws attention to the prospective need for life to take on a different form, down to its everyday details, so that the temporal crisis can be averted. It will not mourn the passing of the time of storytelling. The end of narration, the end of history, does not need to bring about a temporal emptiness. Rather, it opens up the possibility of a life-time that can do without theology and teleology, but which possesses a scent of its own. But this presupposes a revitalization of the *vita contemplativa*.

Not the least cause for today's temporal crisis is the absolute value attached to the *vita activa*. This leads to an *imperative to work*, which degrades the human being into an *animal laborans*. The *hyperkinesia* of everyday life deprives human existence of all contemplative elements and of any capacity for lingering. It leads to a loss of world and time. So-called strategies of deceleration do not overcome this temporal crisis; they even cover up the actual problem. What is necessary is a revitalization of the *vita contemplativa*. The temporal crisis will only be overcome once the *vita activa*, in the midst of its crisis, again incorporates the *vita contemplativa*.

1

Non-Time[1]

... so that in the wavering moment ...
there should be something, at least, that endures.

Friedrich Hölderlin[2]

Nietzsche's 'ultimate man' is remarkably relevant to our present times.[3] 'Health', which is nowadays considered an absolute value – almost a religion – was already 'respect[ed]' by the ultimate man.[4] At the same time, he was also a hedonist. He had his 'little pleasure for the day' and his 'little pleasure for the night'. In him, sense and longing have given way to pleasure and delight: 'What is love? What is creation? What is longing? What is a star? thus asks the Ultimate Man and blinks.'[5] His long, healthy, yet uneventful life finally becomes unbearable to him, and so he turns to drugs, and in the end is killed by drugs: 'A little poison now and then: that produces pleasant dreams. And a lot of poison at last, for a pleasant death.'[6] He seeks to extend his life to infinity through a rigorous politics of health, yet it is paradoxically cut short even before his time has come. Instead of *dying*, he comes to an end in non-time.

Whoever cannot die *at the right time* must perish in non-time. Dying implies that a life comes to its proper end; it is a life's *conclusion*. If life is deprived of every form of meaningful closure, it will be ended in non-time. Dying is difficult in a world in which ending or completion has given way to a passing without end or direction, to a permanent state of being unfinished and beginning anew – in a world, that is, in which individual lives do not terminate in a concrete form or totality, but in which the course of life ends abruptly in non-time.

A general inability to end and to conclude is also the cause of today's acceleration. Time is running off because it cannot find an end or conclusion, because it is not restrained by any temporal gravitational forces. Acceleration is an expression of the bursting of the temporal dam. There are no longer any dams that regulate, articulate or give a rhythm to the flow of time. There are no dams to hold or halt time by giving it something to hold on to – 'hold' in its exquisite double meaning. When time loses all rhythm, when it dissipates into the open without any hold or direction, then all *right* or *good time* also disappears.

Against perishing in non-time, Zarathustra invokes an altogether different kind of death: 'Many die too late and some die too early. Still the doctrine sounds strange: "Die at the right time."/ Die at the right time: thus Zarathustra teaches./ To be sure, he who never lived at the right time could hardly die at the right time!'[7] We humans have altogether lost the sense of the *right time*. The right time gives way to non-time. Death, too, comes in non-time, like a thief: 'But equally hateful to the fighter as to the victor is your grinning death, which comes creeping up like a thief – and yet comes as a master.'[8] It is not possible to fit a freedom unto death within life itself. As opposed to death as a perishing in non-time, what Nietzsche has in mind is a 'consummating death' which actively shapes

2

life itself. Against those 'rope-makers'[9] weaving their long lives, Zarathustra expounds his doctrine of a *free* death: 'I shall show you the consummating death, which shall be a spur and a promise to the living.' This is also precisely Heidegger's idea of 'Being-free for death'. Death is deprived of its non-timeliness by being taken into life and into the present as a shaping and consummating force.[10] The possibility of Nietzsche's free and consummating death, and of Heidegger's Being-free for death, both depend on a temporal gravitation that ensures that the present is framed [*umspannt*], closed round, by the past and future. This temporal tension [*temporale Spannungsverhältnis*] removes the present from its passing without end or direction and infuses it with meaningfulness. The right time, or the right moment, only arises out of the temporal tension within a time that has a direction. In atomized time, by contrast, all temporal points are alike. Nothing distinguishes one point in time from another. The decay of time disperses dying into perishing. Death puts an end to life, life as a directionless sequence of present moments, and it does so in non-time. This is the reason why dying is particularly difficult today. Nietzsche, like Heidegger, opposes the decay of time which de-temporalizes death and turns it into a perishing in non-time:

> He who has a goal and an heir wants death at the time most favourable to his goal and his heir.
>
> And out of reverence for his goal and his heir he will hang up no more withered wreaths in the sanctuary of life.
>
> Truly, I do not want to be like the rope-makers: they spin out their yarn and as a result continually go backwards themselves.[11]

Nietzsche emphatically invokes 'heirs' and 'goals'; he is obviously not fully aware of the full significance of the death of God. For one of its ultimate consequences is the end of history itself – which is to say, the end of 'heirs' and 'goals'. God functions like a stabilizer of time. He ensures a lasting, perennial present. Thus, God's death punctuates time itself, deprives it of any theological, teleological, historical tension [*Spannkraft*]. The present moment shrinks to a fleeting *point* in time, devoid of heirs and free of goals. The present no longer trails things past and future along with it. What Nietzsche undertakes is the difficult attempt to restore temporal tension after the death of God and in light of the approaching end of history. The idea of the 'eternal return of the same' is not just the idea of an *amor fati*: it is precisely an attempt at rehabilitating fate, even at rehabilitating the *time of fate*.

Heidegger's 'they' takes its cue from Nietzsche's ultimate man.[12] The characteristics he attributes to the 'they' also apply neatly to the ultimate man. Nietzsche characterizes him as follows: 'Everyone wants the same thing, everyone is the same: whoever thinks otherwise goes voluntarily into the madhouse.'[13] Heidegger's 'they' is also a temporal phenomenon. The decay of time goes hand in hand with the rise of mass society and increasing uniformity. Authentic existence, the individual in the emphatic sense of the word, is an obstacle to the smooth functioning of the 'they', i.e. of the masses. The acceleration of life prevents the emergence of deviating forms, of things developing and taking on distinct and independent forms. For that to happen, there would need to exist a time of maturation – but this is lacking. In this respect, there is hardly any difference between Nietzsche's 'ultimate man' and Heidegger's 'they'.

Like Nietzsche, Heidegger invokes 'heritage' [*Erbschaft*] and 'tradition' as an antidote to the decay of time into a mere sequence of point-like moments. Everything 'good', he writes, is 'a heritage'. 'Authentic existence' presupposes 'the handing down of a heritage' [*Erbe*].[14] Authentic existence is the 'repetition' which 'makes a *reciprocative rejoinder* to the possibility of

4

that existence which has-been-there'.[15] It is the task of 'herit-age' and 'tradition' to found an historical continuity. Faced with the rapid succession of the 'new', Heidegger invokes the 'old'. His *Being and Time* is an attempt to restore history in the face of its approaching end – more precisely, to restore it as an *empty form*, as a history which simply asserts its temporal formative force, devoid of any content.

Today, things linked to time become obsolete much faster than they used to. They quickly become things of the past, and therefore escape our attention. The present is reduced to a point of currentness. It no longer lasts. Faced with the domi-nation of a point-like, ahistorical present, Heidegger felt that it was necessary to deprive 'the "today" of its character *as pre-sent*'.[16] The cause of the shrinking present, or the disappearing of duration, is not acceleration, as many mistakenly believe.[17] The relationship between the loss of duration and accelera-tion is far more complex than that. Time tumbles on [*stürzt fort*], like an avalanche, precisely because it no longer contains anything to *hold on to* within itself. The tearing away of time,[18] the directionless acceleration of processes (which, *because of the lack of direction*, is no longer really an acceleration at all), is triggered by those point-like presences between which there is no longer any temporal attraction. Acceleration in the proper sense of the word presupposes a course which directs the flow.

Truth itself is a temporal phenomenon. It is a reflection of the lasting, eternal present. The tearing away of time, the shrinking and fleeting present, makes it void. Experience is also based on temporal extension, on interconnections between temporal horizons. For the experiencing subject, what has elapsed has not simply vanished or been discarded. It is, rather, constitutive for the subject's present, for its understanding of itself. A farewell [*Abschied*] does not dilute the presence of the past; it may even make it a deeper presence. What has become part of the past [*das Abgeschiedene*] is therefore not fully cut

5

off [*abgeschnitten*] from the present of experience. Rather, it remains linked up with it. And the subject of experience must be open to what is coming, even to the surprises and the unexpected that the future holds. If it is not, the subject freezes, and becomes a labourer, someone who merely works away time, without changing himself. Changes de-stabilize the process of work. The subject of experience, by contrast, is never identical with itself. It inhabits the transition from past to future. Experience [*Erfahrung*] encompasses a vast temporal space. It is highly time-intensive, as opposed to lived experience [*Erlebnis*], which is point-like and time-poor. Knowledge is as time-intensive as experience. It derives its force from the past as well as from the future. Only through this linking up of temporal horizons does familiarity condense into knowledge. This temporal condensation also distinguishes knowledge from information, which is empty of time, so to speak – timeless in the sense of being deprived of time. Because of this temporal neutrality, information can be stored and arbitrarily retrieved. If things are deprived of memory, they become information or commodities. They are pushed into a time-free, ahistorical space. The storage of information is preceded by the deletion of memory, the deletion of historical time. Where time decays into a mere sequence of point-like presences, it also loses any dialectical tension. Dialectics is in itself an intensive temporal process. Dialectical movement depends on a complex linking up of temporal horizons, i.e. on a *not-yet* of the *already*. What is implicitly present in a particular presence, pulls that presence out of itself and sets it in motion. The motive power of dialectics results from the temporal tension between an already and a not-yet, between a 'having been' and a future. The present within a dialectical process is rich in tension, while today's present lacks all tension.

A present that is reduced to the point of the current moment intensifies non-timeliness at the level of actual behaviour too.

Promising, commitment and fidelity, for instance, are genuinely temporal practices. They bind the future by continuing the present into the future and linking the two, thus creating a temporal continuity that has a stabilizing effect. This continuity protects the future against the violence of non-time. Where the practice of long-term commitment (which is also a form of *conclusion*) gives way to increasing short-termism, non-timeliness also increases, and is reflected at the psychological level in the form of anxiety and restlessness. Growing discontinuity, the atomization of time, destroys the experience of continuity. The world becomes *non-timely*.

The counter-image to time fulfilled is time extended into an empty duration without beginning or end. Empty duration is not opposed to the tearing away of time; it is, rather, a neighbouring phenomenon. It is, so to speak, a silent form, or the negative, of accelerated doing; it is the time that would remain if there were nothing left to do or make, i.e. the temporal form of empty doing. Empty duration and the tearing away of time are consequences of de-temporalization. The restlessness of accelerated doing extends into sleep. It continues at night in the form of the empty duration of sleeplessness:

> Sleepless night: so there is a formula for those tormented hours, drawn out without prospect of end or dawn, in the vain effort to forget time's empty passing. But truly terrifying are the sleepless nights when time seems to contract and run fruitlessly through our hands . . . But what is revealed in such contraction of the hours is the reverse of time fulfilled. If in the latter the power of experience breaks the spell of duration and gathers past and future into the present, in the hasteful sleepless night duration causes unendurable dread.[19]

Adorno's expression 'hasteful sleepless night' is no paradox: haste and empty duration share a common origin. *The haste*

7

of day rules over the night as empty form. Time, now robbed of any hold, any holding gravitation, is running away, is elapsing inexorably. This tearing away of time – time elapsing without a hold – turns the night into an empty duration. Left exposed at the centre of empty duration, no sleep is possible.

Empty duration is a non-articulated, directionless time without any meaningful before or after, remembrance or expectation. In the face of time's infinity, a short human life is a *nothing*. Death is an external power which ends life at non-time. One perishes prematurely at non-time. Death would cease to be a power were it a *conclusion* that follows from life and as the result of a lifetime. Only such a conclusion would make it possible to live one's life to the end on its own terms, and to die at the *right* time. Only temporal forms of conclusion create duration – meaningful and fulfilled time – against a bad infinity. Sleep, too – good sleep – would ultimately be a form of conclusion.

Tellingly, Proust's *À la recherche du temps perdue* begins by saying 'Longtemps, je me suis couché de bonne heure' (For a long time I would go to bed early). In the English translation, the expression 'bonne heure' disappears altogether. These are far-reaching words on time and happiness (bonheur). The *bonne heure*, the good time, is the counter-image to bad infinity, to empty and therefore bad duration in which no sleep is possible. Torn time [*Zeitriß*], the radical discontinuity of time which does not allow for remembrance, leads to a torturous sleeplessness. The first passages of Proust's novel, by contrast, present a gladdening experience of continuity, the *mise en scène* of an effortless hovering between sleeping, dreaming and awakening again, amidst a fluid medium made up of images belonging to memory and perception, a free to-and-fro between the past and present, between solid order and playful confusion. There is no tearing of time that would throw the protagonist into an empty duration. Rather, the sleeper is a player, wanderer and also master of time: 'When a man is asleep, he has in a circle around him the chain of the hours, the sequence of the years, the order of the heavenly bodies.'[20] It is true that occasionally the sleeper also experiences confusion and irritation, but they never end in catastrophe. Rather, 'the good angel of certainty'[21] is there to help:

> when I awoke in the middle of the night, not knowing where I was, I could not even be sure at first who I was, . . . but then the memory . . . would come like a rope let down from heaven to draw me up out of the abyss of not-being,[22] from which I could never have escaped by myself: in a flash I would traverse centuries of civilization, and out of a blurred glimpse of oil-lamps, then of shirts with turned-down collars, would gradually piece together the original components of my ego.[23]

Instead of indifferent and nameless sounds from outside or the excessively loud ticking of a clock, as would be typical for the state of sleeplessness, for empty duration, the sleeper's ears hear something *sonorous*. Even the darkness of night appears colourful and lively like a kaleidoscope: 'I would fall asleep again, and thereafter would reawaken for short snatches only, just long enough to hear the regular creaking of the wainscot, or to open my eyes to stare at the shifting kaleidoscope of the darkness, to savour, in a momentary glimmer of consciousness, the sleep which lay heavy upon the furniture . . .'[24]

It would be erroneous to assume that today's acceleration of life can be explained in terms of the fear of death. This argument roughly goes as follows:

> It was shown that acceleration represents an intuitive solution to the problem of a limited lifetime or the divergence

of the time of the world and the time of life in a secular culture. In this context, the maximal enjoyment of worldly opportunities and the optimal actualization of one's own abilities, and hence the ideal of the *fulfilled life*, has become the paradigm of a successful life. Whoever lives twice as fast can realize twice as many worldly possibilities and thus, as it were, live two lives in the span of one. Whoever becomes infinitely fast approaches the potentially unlimited horizon of the time of the world (and of worldly possibilities) within one lifetime to the extent that she can realize a plurality of life possibilities in a single earthly lifespan. She therefore no longer needs to fear death, the annihilator of options.[25]

The idea is that whoever lives twice as fast can enjoy twice as many life possibilities; the acceleration of life multiplies life and thus brings a person closer to the goal of having a fulfilled life. But this is a naïve calculation which rests on a confusion of fulfilment with mere plenitude. A fulfilled life cannot be explained on a quantitative basis. It does not result from a plenitude of life possibilities, just as a recounting or listing of events does not necessarily amount to a narration or account. Rather, the latter require a special synthesis to which they owe their meaning. A long list of events does not produce the tension which characterizes a story, while a very short story may nevertheless possess a powerful narrative tension. And, thus, a very short life can also achieve the ideal of a fulfilled life. The acceleration thesis does not recognize that the real problem today is the fact that life has lost the possibility of reaching a meaningful *conclusion*. It is this fact that leads to the hectic rush and nervousness which characterize contemporary life. One begins ever anew; one zaps through 'life possibilities', precisely because of an inability to bring any single possibility to a conclusion. The individual's life is not informed by a story or meaningful totality. It is misleading to talk of an acceleration of life pursued with the aim of maximizing its possibilities. Upon closer scrutiny, this acceleration turns out to be a nervous restlessness which makes life whizz, so to speak; it hurtles from one possibility to the next. It never achieves rest – that is, completion.

A further contemporary problem with respect to dying is the radical individualization or atomization of life, which intensifies its finite character. Life loses more and more of the breadth that would give it duration; it contains little of the world. This atomization of life renders it radically mortal. It is above all this particular mortality which causes a general restlessness and urgency. This nervousness may appear to indicate a general acceleration. But in reality what we see is not a real acceleration of life. Rather, all that has happened is that life has become more rushed, less perspicuous and more directionless. Because of its dissipation, time no longer exerts an ordering force. Thus, formative or decisive caesuras are absent from life. The time of a life is no longer structured by sections, completions, thresholds and transitions. Instead, there is a rush from one present to the next and an aging without growing old. Finally, one perishes in non-time. This is what today makes dying more difficult than ever.

2

Time without a Scent

Because nowhere now
An immortal is to be seen in the skies . . .[1]

Friedrich Hölderlin

The mythical world is full of meaning. Gods are nothing but eternal bearers of meaning. They make the world meaningful and significant, let it make sense. They tell us about the way things and events are related to each other, and these narrated connections create sense. Out of nothing, narration makes *world*. Full of gods means full of meaning, full of narration. The world becomes readable, like a *picture*. You need only let your gaze move here, move there, in order to read the sense, the meaningful order, off it. Everything has its place – that is, its meaning – within a firmly set order (the *cosmos*). If anything moves from its proper place, it is put right again. Time *sets it right*.[2] Time is order. Time is justice. If a human individual shifts things arbitrarily, this is an offence, and time will atone for it, thus restoring the eternal order. Time is just (*diké*).

Events take place in fixed relations with each other; they form meaningful chains. No event is allowed to step out of line. Every event reflects the eternal, unchanging substance of the world. Here, there are no movements that modify the valid order. In this world of eternal recurrence, acceleration would make no sense at all. Only the eternal repetition of the same, even the reproduction of what was, of eternal truth, makes sense. Thus, prehistoric man lives in a lasting present.

The historical world is altogether different. It is not simply given as a completed *picture* that reveals an eternal substance, an unchanging order, to the onlooker. Events are no longer arranged on a static *plane*, but on a progressive *line*. The time which links events, and thereby releases meanings, passes in a linear fashion, and it is not the return of the same but the possibility of change that makes it meaningful. Everything takes place as a process, which means either progress or decay. Historical time releases meaning in the sense that it is *directed*. The temporal line has a direction, a syntax.

Historical time knows no lasting present. Things do not remain arranged in an immutable order. Time is not leading back but leading forwards; it is not bringing back but collecting.[3] The past and the future drift apart. What makes time meaningful is not its sameness but its difference. Time is change, process, development. The present has no substance of its own; it is only a transitional point. Nothing *is*. Everything *becomes*. Everything changes. The repetition of the same gives way to the event. Movements and changes do not create chaos, but another, a new kind of order. Temporal meaningfulness is based in the future. This orientation towards the future produces a forward temporal pull that *may* also have accelerating effects.

Historical time is a linear time which can, however, pass or appear in very different forms. The time of eschatology differs greatly from the kind of historical time that promises progress. Eschatological time, as the final time, refers to the end of the world. The eschaton marks the beginning of the end of time, the end of history itself. And a thrownness characterizes the human being's relationship with the future. Eschatological time does not allow for any action, any projection. The human individual is not free; it is subjected to God. It does not project *itself* into the future. It does not project *its* time. Rather, it is thrown into the end, into the final end of world and time. It is not the subject of history. Rather, it is God who judges.

Originally, the concept of 'revolution' also had an entirely different meaning from the one associated with it now. Although it signified a process, it was not free from connotations of return and repetition. Originally, *revolutio* referred to the orbits of the stars. Applied to history, it signifies the fact that the forms of domination, which are limited in number, reoccur in cyclical fashion. The changes which take place in the course of history are integrated into a cycle. It is not progress but repetition that characterizes the historical process. Neither is the human being a free subject of history. Not freedom, but thrownness continues to determine the human relationship to time. It is not humans who make revolutions; rather, they are subjected to them, just as they are subjected to the laws of the stars. Time is characterized by natural constants. Time is facticity.[4]

During the time of the Enlightenment, a particular idea of historical time emerged. As opposed to the eschatological idea of time it assumes an open-ended future. Here, temporality is not dominated by its being towards an end, but by the departure into the new. And temporality acquires a significance, a weight of its own. There is no helpless, headlong rush towards the apocalyptic end. And no facticity and no natural constants force temporality to take the form of circular repetition. This gives an altogether different meaning to the concept of revolution, one free from the association with stellar orbits. The linear, progressive course of events now determines the temporality of revolution, rather than circular orbits.

The notion of temporality that developed during the Enlightenment freed itself of thrownness and facticity. Time was rendered *non-factual* as well as being *de-naturalized*; it is now freedom which determines the human relationship to time. The human being is neither thrown into the end of time, nor into the natural circulation of things. What animates history is the idea of freedom, the idea of the 'progress of human reason'.[5] The subject of time is no longer a judging God, but a free human being that projects *itself* towards the future. Time is not fate but *projection*. The human relation with the future is determined not by thrownness but by feasibility. The human being is the one that *makes (produire)* the revolution. Thus, concepts like revolutionizing and revolutionary, which point towards feasibility, become possible. But the idea of feasibility de-stabilizes the world, and even de-stabilizes time itself. That God which, as the source of an eternal present, had long had a stabilizing effect, now slowly takes its leave from time.

The remarkable burst of innovation in the natural sciences that began in the sixteenth century was triggered by a belief in feasibility. Technological improvements are made at ever-shorter intervals. Bacon's dictum 'knowledge is power' precisely reflects the belief that the world can be made. The political revolution and the Industrial Revolution are connected, both being animated and advanced by the same belief. An entry on railways in the Brockhaus encyclopedia of 1838 conjoins the two in heroic tones: the railway is transfigured into a '*Dampftriumphwagen*' [steam-powered triumph engine] of the revolution.[6]

Revolution in the age of the Enlightenment is based on

a time rendered non-factual. Freed of all thrownness and of all natural or theological coercion, time, like that colossal engine, is unleashed towards the future, which is expected to bring salvation. This time inherits the teleological character of the eschatological idea of time. History remains the history of salvation. Given the fact that the goal is in the future, the acceleration of the historical process now makes sense. Thus, at the constitutional ceremony in 1793, Robespierre said: 'Les progrès de la raison humaine ont preparé cette grande revolution, et c'est à vous qu'est specialement imposé le devoir de l'accélérer.' [The progress of human reason prepared this great revolution, and you especially are charged with the duty of accelerating it.][7]

Not God but the free human being is the master of time. Having been freed of its thrownness, the human being projects what is to come. But this *regime change* from God to human is not without consequences. It *de-stabilizes time* because God is the authority which confers finality and the seal of eternal truth upon the prevailing order. God stands for a lasting present. With the regime change, time loses this *hold*, which had created a resistance to change. Büchner's drama on the French Revolution, *Danton's Death*, gives expression to this experience when Camille proclaims: 'The ordinary delusions that people call "sanity" are all so unbearably boring. The luckiest man of them all was the one that imagined he was God the father, God the son and God the Holy Ghost.'[8]

Historical time *can* rush ahead because it does not rest in itself, because its centre of gravity is not in the present. It does permit any genuine lingering. Any lingering only delays the progressive process. No duration *comports* time. Time is meaningful insofar as it moves towards a goal. Hence, acceleration makes sense. However, due to the meaningfulness of time, it is not perceived as such. What is noticed most of all is the *meaning* of history. Acceleration is felt as such only where time loses its historical meaningfulness, its sense. Acceleration becomes topical or problematic as such precisely at the moment when time is torn away into a meaningless future.

Mythical time is restful, like a *picture*. Historical time, by contrast, has the form of a *line* which runs or rushes towards a goal. If this line loses its narrative or teleological tension, it disintegrates into *points* which *whizz around* without any sense of direction. The end of history atomizes time into point-time. Myth once gave way to history: the static picture turned into a progressive line. Now, *history* gives way to *information*. The latter does not possess any narrative width or breadth. It is neither centred, nor does it have a direction. Information falls down on us, so to speak. History clears, selects, channels the tangle of events and forces them on to a linear narrative track. The disappearance of this track leads to a proliferation of information and events which whizz around without direction. Information *has no scent*. In this, it differs from history. As opposed to Baudrillard's thesis, information does not relate to history like an ever more perfect simulation to the original or origin.[9] Rather, information represents a new paradigm. An altogether different temporality is inherent in information. It is a phenomenon of atomized time, namely of point-time.

Between points there necessarily yawns an emptiness, an empty interval in which nothing happens, in which no *sensation* takes place. In mythical and historical time, by contrast, no emptiness emerges, because neither picture nor line is interrupted by intervals; both of these form a narrative continuum. Only points allow empty in-between spaces to appear. These intervals in which nothing happens cause boredom [*Langeweile*]. Or they appear threatening, because where nothing happens and where intentionality can find no object, there is death. Thus, point-time produces the compulsion

17

to remove, or to shorten, the empty intervals. Attempts are made to let the *sensations* follow each other in quicker succession, in order to keep the empty intervals from *lasting long* [*lange weilen*]. Consequently, the acceleration of the sequence of cuts or events is intensified to the point of hysteria, and it takes hold of all areas of life. Due to the lack of narrative tension, atomized time cannot hold our attention for long. Thus, the senses are constantly provided with new or drastic perceptions. Point-time does not permit any contemplative lingering.

Atomized time is a discontinuous time. There is nothing to bind events together and thus found a connection, a duration. The senses are therefore confronted with the unexpected and sudden, which, in turn, produces a diffuse feeling of anxiety. Atomization, individualization and the experience of discontinuity are also responsible for various forms of violence. Today, those social structures which create continuity and duration are increasingly disintegrating. Atomization and individualization take hold of societies as a whole. Social practices such as promising, fidelity or commitment, which are temporal practices in the sense that they commit to a future and thus limit the horizon of the future, thus founding duration, are all losing their importance.

Mythical and historical time possess a narrative tension. They are formed by a specific interlinking of events. The narration gives time a scent. Point-time, by contrast, is a time without scent. Time begins to emit a scent when it gains duration; when it is given a narrative or deep tension; when it gains depth and breadth, even *space*. Time loses its scent when it is divested of all deep structure or sense, when it is atomized or when it flattens out, thins out or shortens. If it detaches entirely from the anchoring which holds, even inhibits [*verhält*], it, then it becomes devoid of all support [*haltlos*]. Taken out of its mount [*Halterung*], so to speak, it rushes off [*stürzt*

18

fort]. Acceleration, much discussed today, is not a primary process which subsequently leads to various changes within the lifeworld, but a symptom, a secondary process, that is, a *consequence* of time having lost its hold and having been atomized, its being without any inhibiting gravitation. Time rushes off [*stürzt fort*], even is in precipitous haste [*überstürzt sich*], in order to compensate for an essential *lack of being*. In this, however, it is not successful, because acceleration by itself does not produce any *hold*. On the contrary, it only makes the existing lack of being more pungent.

3

The Speed of History

La vie serait une suite ininterrompue
de sensations que rien ne lierait.[1]

Denis Diderot

Modern technology moves the human being away from the
earth. Aeroplanes and spaceships pull the human being away
from the earth's gravitational field. The further one moves
away from the earth, the smaller it gets. And the faster one
moves on the earth, the more it shrinks. Every removal of distance on the earth brings with it an increasing distancing of
the human being from the earth, thus estranging the human
being from it. The internet and electronic mail let geography,
even the earth itself, disappear. Electronic mail carries no mark
indicating the place from which it was sent; it is without a space.
Modern technology *de-terrestrializes* human life. Heidegger's
philosophy of 'autochthony' [*Bodenständigkeit*] is an attempt at
re-terrestrializing and *re-factualizing* the human being.

Jean Baudrillard elucidates the end of history with the

20

image of a body which, through acceleration, frees itself from the earth's gravitational pull:

> Staying with this image, one might suppose that the acceleration of modernity, of technology, events and media, of all exchanges – economic, political and sexual – has propelled us to 'escape velocity', with the result that we have flown free of the referential sphere of the real end of history.[2]

According to Baudrillard, a 'degree of slowness' is needed in order for events to condense or crystallize into history. His image of the accelerating body suggests the conclusion that it is exactly acceleration that is responsible for the end of history, that acceleration is the cause of the loss of meaning that is threatening us. The slipstream of acceleration, according to his 'plausible' hypothesis, hurls things out of the referential space that gives them meaning. They decay into fragments, into isolated particles of the real which whizz around in a space devoid of meaning. An enormous kinetic energy, whose origin remains hidden, pulls things out of their orbits, that is, out of their meaningful contexts:

> Once beyond this gravitational effect, which keeps bodies in orbit, all the atoms of meaning get lost in space. Each atom pursues its own trajectory to infinity and is lost in space. This is precisely what we are seeing in our present-day societies, intent as they are on accelerating all bodies, messages, and processes in all directions ... Every political, historical and cultural fact possesses a kinetic energy which wrenches it from its own space and propels it into a hyperspace where ... it loses all meaning.[3]

The image of atoms propelled outwards in all directions by the slipstream of acceleration, and thus pulled out of their contexts of meaning, is not entirely apposite. It suggests a one-sided causal connection between acceleration and loss of meaning. But although a possible interaction between acceleration and a vacuum of meaning cannot be disputed, the assumption of a 'particle acceleration which has smashed the referential orbit of things once and for all'[4] is questionable.

Acceleration is not the only possible explanation for the disappearance of meaning. We may also think of an altogether different image: the earth's gravitational field, which keeps things in their fixed orbits, slowly disappears. Freed of their contexts of meaning, the things begin to hover or whizz around without direction. From the outside, this might look as though things were freeing themselves from the earth's gravitational field with the help of acceleration. But in reality they would be escaping the earth and moving away from each other because of the absence of the *gravitation of meaning*. It is also misleading to talk of 'atoms of meaning', because meaning is not atomic. Only meaningless violence can emanate from atoms. It is only as a result of the absence of gravitation that things are individualized into atoms devoid of meaning. They are no longer kept in those orbits which integrate them into contexts of meaning. Thus, they decay into atoms and whizz around in a meaningless 'hyperspace'. In this scenario, the loss of meaning does not result from an 'escape velocity' which propels the things out of the 'referential sphere of the real end of history', but from the absence or weakness of gravitation. The missing gravitational force brings forth a new condition, a new constellation of being, from which the various phenomena characterizing the present day are to be derived. Acceleration is *only one of them*. The disappearance of the orbits of things, which give them a direction, and thus meaning, can also be shown to be responsible for a phenomenon that is the opposite of acceleration, namely the stasis of things. Baudrillard himself notes that not only acceleration but also slowness can lead to the end of history:

> Matter slows the passing of time. To put it more precisely, time at the surface of a very dense body seems to be going in slow motion . . . This inert matter of the social is not produced by a lack of exchanges, information or communication, but by the multiplication and saturation of exchanges. It is the product of the hyperdensity of cities, commodities, messages and circuits. It is the cold star of the social and, around that mass, history is also cooling . . . It will eventually come to a stop and be extinguished like light and time in the vicinity of an infinitely dense mass. . .[5]

In this passage, Baudrillard again connects the end of history with the question of speed. Too fast or too slow a speed of social and economic circulation means that history disappears. Accordingly, history, or the production of meaning, presupposes a particular speed of exchange processes, which must be neither too fast nor too slow. A speed that is too fast dissipates meaning. A speed that is too slow, by contrast, leads to blockages which suffocate all movement.

However, in reality history is not sensitive to changes in the speed of social and economic exchange processes. Speed *by itself* does not have such a great influence on the historical production of meaning. Rather, it is the instability of the orbits, the disappearing gravitation itself, which causes temporal irritation or oscillation. The latter consist *not only of acceleration, but also of deceleration.* Things accelerate because they have no hold, because nothing keeps them in a stable orbit. The specificity of the orbit consists in it being selective, in the fact that only certain things may be caught in it because it is narrow. If this narrative orbit of history decays completely, there is *also* a massification of events and information.

Everything pushes into the present, leading to blockages, which have a decelerating effect. Such blockages are not the result of acceleration. The disappearance of selective orbits precisely does not lead to a massification of events and information. Although Baudrillard realized that the end of history is connected not only to acceleration, but also to deceleration, he nevertheless makes speed directly responsible for the loss of meaning. Baudrillard and many others overlook the fact that acceleration and deceleration are two different phenomena arising from a process at a deeper level. Thus it is erroneously assumed that stasis is a *consequence* of general acceleration:

> The two diagnoses of time that appear so contradictory, social acceleration and social rigidity, are only at first glance contradictory to one another. In the memorable metaphor of a 'frenetic standstill' (*rasender Stillstand*) . . . they are synthesized into a *posthistoire* diagnosis in which the *rush* of historical events only provides scant cover for (and ultimately, in effect, produces) a standstill . . .[6]

According to this problematic thesis, deceleration and standstill 'represent an internal element and an inherent complementary principle of the acceleration process itself'.[7] This thesis erroneously postulates a 'dialectical inversion of acceleration and movement into rigidity and standstill'.[8] But the phenomenon of standstill does not arise from the fact that everyone wants to run at the same time, that all levers are activated at the same time; it is not the 'flip side' of the process of acceleration.[9] It does not have the acceleration of movements and actions as its cause, but precisely the *no-longer-knowing-where-to-go* of movements and actions. This lack of direction leads to phenomena that, at first sight, seem contrary to it: acceleration and standstill. They are the two sides of the same coin.

The general de-temporalization leads to the disappearance of temporal sections and caesurae, the thresholds and transitions which create meaning. The feeling that time passes more quickly now than before is also due to the absence of a pronounced articulation of time. This feeling is intensified by the fact that events follow each other in quick succession without leaving lasting traces, without becoming *experiences*. Because of the missing gravitation, things are encountered only fleetingly. Nothing carries weight. Nothing is *incisive*, nothing final. There are no incisions. When it is no longer possible to decide what is of importance, then everything loses importance. Due to the excessive number of possible connections, i.e. possible directions, things are rarely ever completed. Completion requires a structured, organic time. Within an open and endless process, by contrast, nothing is ever completed. Incompletion becomes a permanent condition.

Theories which declare acceleration to be a major driving force of modernity are problematic. Everywhere they suspect an increase in speed. They believe that they can also detect an increasing acceleration in the literature of modernity, where it finds expression in the form of an increasing narrative tempo:

> time flows faster and faster as the novel progresses so that the same number of pages recount a few hours of narrated time at the beginning of the book that later portray days and then weeks, until by the end of the work months and years are compressed into a few pages.[10]

The assumption of a gradual increase of narrative tempo has its source in a partial and one-sided perception, because, paradoxically, this increase goes hand in hand with a slowing down of the narrative tempo, which is nearing a standstill. The common root of acceleration *and* slowing down is a *narrative de-temporalization.* They are different manifestations of the *same* process. The exclusive focus on acceleration obscures this process, which also becomes manifest in the form of standstill and deceleration.

Due to this de-temporalization, there is no narrative progress. The narrator dwells upon each and every minor and insignificant event because of an inability to *distinguish* between what is important and what is unimportant. Narration requires distinction and selection. Michel Butor's novel *L'emploi du temps* [*Passing Time*] exemplifies this narrative crisis, which is also a temporal crisis. The slowness of the narration results from the narrator's inability to structure what happens by way of meaning-creating incision and sectioning. Due to the absence of a selective narrative path, the narrator cannot decide what is of importance. The narration loses all rhythm. The inertia *and* hastiness of the narration are both symptoms of the lack of narrative tension.[11] The narration cannot find a rhythm that would allow for a *harmonious alternation of slowness and acceleration.* Narrative rhythm presupposes a closed time. Temporal dissipation [*Zerstreuung*] does not permit any collection, any gathering of events into a closed wholeness; it leads to temporal leaps and oscillations. The disorganized mass of events effects an acceleration *as well as* a slowing down of the narrative tempo. Where the mass of events pushes into the present, the narration rushes off without a hold. Where it dissolves into a general indifference, the narration becomes sluggish. Due to the absence of mastery over the mass of events, the narration loses all sense of orientation and all rhythm. Both the acceleration and the slowing down of the narration result from the lack of a rhythmic pace.

De-temporalization leads to the disappearance of all narrative tension. Narrated time disintegrates into a mere chronology of events. Thus, the text lists rather than narrates, and the events do not condense into a coherent picture.

This inability to produce a narrative synthesis, which is also an incapacity for temporal synthesis, calls forth a crisis of identity. The narrator is no longer able to collect the events around *him*. The temporal dissipation [*Zerstreuung*] destroys any kind of collecting, and thus the narrator cannot establish a stable identity for himself. The temporal crisis is an identity crisis. Due to the lack of narrative suspense, it is also not possible to conclude the story in a meaningful way. It drags itself along from event to event without making any genuine progress and without reaching any destination. It can only be broken off abruptly. Breaking off in non-time replaces a meaningful end. In the case of *L'emploi du temps*, a departure comes to the rescue. The narration breaks off in non-time:

> . . . and I haven't even time to set down something that happened on the evening of February 29th, something that seemed very important and that I shall forget as I move farther away from you, Bleston, as you lie dying, Bleston, whose dying embers I have fanned, for now the long minute hand stands upright and my departure closes this last sentence.[12]

4

From the Age of Marching to the Age of Whizzing

He who will one day teach men to fly will
have moved all boundary-stones; all boundary-stones
will themselves fly into the air to him, he will
baptize the earth anew – as 'the weightless'.

Friedrich Nietzsche[1]

According to Zygmunt Bauman, the modern human is a pilgrim who wanders the world as though it were a desert, giving form to the formless, continuity to the episodic, and producing a whole out of the fragmentary.[2] The modern pilgrim practises a 'living-towards-projects'; the pilgrim's world is 'directional'.[3] The way Bauman uses the expression 'pilgrim' does not fully fit with the situation of the modern human. The *peregrinus* feels a stranger in this world: he or she is not at home *Here*, and is thus always on the way to a *There*. In modernity, it is precisely this difference between Here and There which disappears. The modern human does not progress towards a There, but towards a better or different

Here. For the *peregrinus*, by contrast, there is no progress associated with a Here. Further, his path is neither 'orderly' nor 'secure'. Rather, the desert is uncertain and insecure. As opposed to the pilgrim who follows a prescribed path, the modern human creates a path him- or herself. He or she is more like a soldier who marches towards a goal, or like a labourer. The *peregrinus* is thrown into its facticity. The modern human, by contrast, is free.

Modernity is a time of de-factualization and freedom. It frees itself from the thrownness whose thrower or projector is called God. De-factualization and secularization rest on the same premises. The human being elevates itself to become the subject of history, confronted by the world as an object that can be produced. Production takes the place of repetition. Freedom is not defined on the basis of facticity. In pre-modern times, by contrast, the human being followed a pre-given path, which, like the orbits of the heavenly bodies, repeated itself eternally. The pre-modern human found things which he or she accepted or suffered, into which he or she was thrown: a human being characterized by facticity and repetition.

Although modernity is no longer based on a theological narrative, secularization does not lead to a de-narrativization of the world. Modernity remains a narrative age, where the narrative is one of history as progress and development. This age, with its gaze turned towards the immanent world, expects a salvation that lies in the future. The narrative of progress or freedom bestows meaning and significance upon time itself. In light of the goal it expects to reach, acceleration makes sense, and is desirable; it can easily be incorporated into the narrative. Thus, technological progress is underpinned by a quasi-religious narrative which assigns it the function of accelerating the arrival of a future salvation. The railway, for instance, is hallowed as a time machine which lets the present catch up faster with the expected future:

On iron rails our century rolls towards a bright and glorious aim. We shall cover the spiritual distance we travel on it in even faster flight than we do physical spaces! And we hope that just as the colossal rolling steam engines smash any external obstacle that insolently and foolhardily attempts to block their path, any spiritual obstacle set up by envy and prejudice will likewise be smashed by their colossal power. The steam-powered triumph engine is still only at the beginning of its journey and therefore only rolls slowly! This alone is the reason for the mistaken and blinded hope it might be possible to stop it. But in the course of its rolling, the wings of its speed grow and overpower those who try to throw a spanner in its wheels of fate.[4]

The author of this Brockhaus article connected the telos of a 'self-determined humanity' to technological progress. The railway is a machine for acceleration which serves the purpose of realizing the sacred goal of humanity faster: 'Although the course of history aimed at this truly divine goal from time immemorial, it will reach it centuries earlier on the rolling wheels of the railways storming ahead.' History as the history of salvation survives secularization in the form of an inner-worldly story of progress. The inner-worldly hope for happiness and freedom takes the place of religious expectations of divine salvation.

The intentionality of modernity is a projecting. It is goal-oriented. Thus, its form of moving is a marching towards a goal. A leisurely stroll or a directionless floating does not correspond to its nature. The only commonality between the modern human and the pilgrim is determination. The firm steps which need to be synchronized and accelerated are what count. It is precisely the teleology of progress, that is, the difference between the present and future, which produces the pressure to accelerate. Seen this way, acceleration

30

is characteristic of modernity. It presupposes a linear process. Acceleration does not add a new quality to directionless movements which have no identifiable goal.

After modernity, or in postmodernity, entirely different forms of movement emerge due to the absence of a teleology. There is no longer a comprehensive horizon, no all-pervading goal to which one should *march*. Zygmunt Bauman therefore declares the pace of the flâneur and the vagabond to be characteristic of postmodernity. But today's society not only lacks the leisureliness of the flâneur, it also lacks the hovering lightness of the vagabond. Haste, franticness, restlessness, nervousness and a diffuse sense of anxiety determine today's life. Instead of leisurely strolling around, one rushes from one event to another. This haste and restlessness characterize neither the flâneur nor the vagabond. It is therefore problematic that Bauman uses 'strolling' and 'zapping' almost synonymously. They are both meant to be expressions of a postmodern absence of ties and of commitments: 'The ultimate freedom is screen-directed, lived in the company of surfaces, and called *zapping*.'[5] This statement assumes a highly problematic concept of freedom. To be free does not simply mean to be un-tied or un-committed. It is not the 'release from' something or dis-embeddedness which makes us free, but inclusion and embeddedness. The total lack of relationships causes anxiousness and worry. The Indo-European root *fri*, from which terms such as 'free', 'peace' or 'quietude' [*Friede*], and 'friend' are derived, means 'to love'. Thus, 'free' originally meant 'pertaining to friends or loved ones'. One feels free in relationships of love and friendship. It is not the absence of ties, but ties themselves which set us free. Freedom is a word which pertains to relations par excellence. Without *hold* there is no freedom.

Because of the lack of hold, life today finds it hard to get a grip. Temporal dissipation throws it off balance. *It whizzes*.

There are no stable social rhythms or cycles to unburden the individual's temporal economy. Not everyone is capable of independently defining their own time. The increasing plurality of temporal sequences irritates the individual human being and asks too much of it. The lack of pre-given temporal structures does not lead to an increase in freedom, but to a lack of orientation.

The temporal dissipation in postmodernity is a consequence of a paradigm change which cannot exclusively be explained in terms of the intensified acceleration of the life and production processes. Acceleration in the proper sense is a genuinely *modern* phenomenon. It assumes a linear, teleological development. The theory of modernity, which elevates acceleration to the status of the main driving force behind all changes in social structures, and which thus attempts to explain the structural transformations in postmodernity with the logic of acceleration, is based on false premises. The drama of acceleration is a phenomenon of the previous centuries. We may call it a drama to the extent that it is accompanied by a narrative. De-narrativization also de-dramatizes the accelerated directed process [*Fortlauf*] into a *directionless whizzing*. The drama of acceleration comes to its end, not least because the speed of the transmission of events and information has reached the speed of light.

It is erroneously assumed that the forms of social organization which were characteristic of modernity, and which served the purpose of accelerating the processes of production and exchange, have given way to postmodern forms of organization because they inhibited further acceleration:

> It seems that the dynamic forces of acceleration themselves produce the institutions and forms of practice they need in accordance with the respective requirements of their further unfolding and then annihilate them again upon reaching

the speed limits those forms have made possible. From this perspective . . . it appears that it is the increase of speed . . . that is the real driving force of (modern) history.[6]

The stable personal identity, for instance, which during modern times served the purpose of making exchange processes more dynamic, is, this thesis holds, abandoned again once a certain speed is reached because of its lack of flexibility. Accordingly, all those changes in social structures, such as atomization and the erosion of institutions, which took place in the wake of modernity, or in postmodernity, are a direct consequence of the intensified processes of acceleration during modernity. Thus, the assumption is 'that for temporal–structural reasons modernity in fact finds itself in a transition to a phase that is *posthistorical* and hence *post-political* in a specific sense'.[7] According to this problematic thesis, postmodern de-narrativization is solely the result of an intensified acceleration of the life and production processes. In reality, the reverse is the case: the lack of temporal gravitation is what throws life off balance. When life loses all rhythm, temporal disturbances occur. One of the symptoms of de-narrativization is the vague feeling that life itself is accelerating, while in reality nothing is accelerating. When looking more closely, what we find is a feeling of being rushed. Genuine acceleration requires a directed process, but de-narrativization yields an undirected, directionless movement, a whizzing which is indifferent towards acceleration. Because of the reduction in narrative tension, events whizz around without direction; they are no longer steered on to narrative paths.

When we are constantly asked to begin anew, to choose a new option or version of something, we may get the impression that life is accelerating. In reality, what we face is an absence of any experience of duration. If a process that is continuous and determined by a narrative logic is accelerated, then this acceleration does not impress itself *as such* on perception. To a large extent, it is absorbed by the narrative meaning of the process and not itself perceived as disturbing or stressful. The impression that time moves considerably faster than before also has its origin in the fact that today we are unable to *linger*, that the experience of duration has become so rare. It is mistakenly assumed that the feeling of being rushed is the result of a 'fear of missing out':

> The fear of missing (valuable) things and therefore the desire to heighten the pace of life are . . . the result of a cultural program that began developing in early modernity and consists in making one's own life more fulfilled and richer in experience through an accelerating savouring of worldly options, i.e. by escalating the rate of experience and thereby realizing a 'good life'. The cultural *promise of acceleration* lies in this idea. As a result subjects want to live faster.[8]

But in actual fact the very opposite is the case. Whoever tries to live faster, will ultimately also die faster. It is not the total number of events, but the experience of duration which makes life more fulfilling. Where one event follows close on the heels of another, nothing enduring comes about. Fulfilment and meaning cannot be explained on quantitative grounds. A life that is lived quickly, without anything lasting long and without anything slow, a life that is characterized by quick, short-term and short-lived experiences is itself a *short* life, no matter how high the 'rate of experience' may be.

What will the *pace of the future* be? The age of the pilgrimage and of marching are definitely over. Will the human being, after a short period of whizzing, return to the earth as a *walker*? Or will the human being leave behind the weightiness of the earth and of work altogether, and discover the lightness of hovering, of a hovering wandering with leisure, in other words, the *scent of hovering time*?

5

The Paradox of the Present

'Does that come to pass?' – 'No, it doesn't.'
– 'Something comes, however.'
– 'In waiting that stops and leaves all coming behind.'

Maurice Blanchot[1]

Intervals or thresholds form part of the topology of *passion*. They are zones of forgetting, of loss, of death, of fear and anxiety, but also of longing, of hope, of adventure, of promising and expecting. In many respects, an interval is also a source of suffering and of pain. Remembering becomes a passion if it battles against time's surrendering of the past to oblivion. From this perspective, Proust's novel on time is a passion story. Waiting becomes passion if the temporal interval which separates the present from the expected future expands into the open. Waiting creates suffering if the coming to be of what is expected or has been promised, namely the moment of the final possession of it or of the final arrival, is delayed.

The temporal interval stretches between two conditions or events. The meantime is a transitional time in which the one occupying it is in no definite condition. There is nothing which defines this in-between. The excess of indistinctness creates a feeling of restlessness and anxiety, in other words a threshold feeling. What is worrying and frightening is the transition towards the unknown. Hesitation is the form of movement at the threshold. Timidity is also part of the threshold feeling. The time between departure and arrival is an uncertain time during which we must reckon with the incalculable. But it is also a time of hope or expectation, which prepares the arrival.

The *path* which separates the place of departure from the place of arrival is also an interval. Like *place* itself, it is semantically rich. The path of a pilgrimage, for instance, is not an empty space between two places that is to be traversed as quickly as possible. Rather, it constitutes the very goal to be reached. Being-on-one's-way here is altogether meaningful. The walking means doing penance, healing or gratefulness. It is a prayer. The pilgrim's path is not merely a thoroughfare, but a transition to a *There*. In temporal terms, the pilgrim is on the way to the future, which is expected to bring salvation. To that extent, he is not a *tourist*. A *transition* is an alien notion to a tourist for whom everywhere is *Here and Now*. A tourist is not *on the way* in the proper sense. Paths are impoverished, turned into empty thoroughfares that would not be *worth seeing*. The totalization of Here and Now divests the in-between spaces of any meaning. Today's experience is characterized by the fact that it is very poor in transitions.

If the goal is the sole point of orientation, then the spatial interval to be crossed before reaching it is simply an obstacle to be overcome as quickly as possible. Pure orientation towards the goal deprives the in-between space of all meaning, emptying it to become a corridor without any value of its own. Acceleration is the attempt to make the temporal interval that is needed for bridging the spatial interval disappear altogether. The rich meaning of the path disappears. Acceleration leads to a semantic impoverishment of the world. Space and time no longer *mean* very much.

Once the spatio-temporal interval is perceived exclusively under the negative aspect of loss, there will be efforts to make it disappear altogether. Electronic memories and other technological possibilities for recurrence destroy the temporal interval which is responsible for forgetting. They make what is past instantaneously retrievable and available. Nothing must evade this instantaneous access. The intervals which work against instantaneity are removed. Electronic mail produces instantaneity by destroying the paths as spatial intervals in their entirety. It dispenses with space itself. Intervals are destroyed in order to produce total proximity and simultaneity. Any remoteness, any distance, is removed. The aim is to make everything available in the Here and Now. Instantaneity becomes passion.

Whatever cannot be rendered present does not exist. Everything has to be present. In-between spaces and in-between times, which have the effect of *removing presence*, are abolished. There are only two conditions left: nothing and the present. There is no in-between any more. But *being* is more than being-present. Human life is impoverished when all forms of in-between are removed from it. Human culture is also rich in in-betweens. Celebrations often give form to the in-between. Thus, for instance, advent time is an in-between time, a time of waiting.

The totalization of the Here removes the *There*. The nearness of the Here destroys the aura of distance. The thresholds which separate the There from the Here, the visible from the invisible, the alien from the familiar, all disappear. The absence of thresholds results from the compulsion to make everything visible and available. Any There disappears in a side-by-side of events, sensations and information that has no gaps. Everything is Here. The There is no longer of any importance. The human being is no longer a *threshold creature*. Yes, thresholds cause suffering and passion, but they also *delight*.

The effect of intervals is not only that they delay. They also have the function of ordering and structuring. Without intervals there is only an unstructured, directionless side-by-side or confusion of events. Intervals structure not only perception, but also life. Transitions and sections provide life with a direction, hence with meaning. The elimination of intervals produces a space without directions. As there is no well-defined section in such a space, it is also impossible to complete a specific phase that would form part of a meaningful sequence. Where events follow each other in quick succession, there is also no resolve to reach completion. In a space without direction it is possible to end a course of action at any time, and to begin a new one instead. Given numerous possibilities for further connections, completion does not make a lot of sense. Whoever completes may miss the connection.[2] A space made up of possibilities for further connection does not have any continuity. In it, again and again, decisions are made anew, and new possibilities are constantly pursued, making time discontinuous. No decision is final. Decisions, once made, have to give way to new decisions. What is suspended is linear, irreversible time, namely that of destiny.

The internet space is a space without direction. It is woven from possible connections, or links, which do not fundamentally differ from each other. No direction or option has an absolute priority over the others. Ideally, a change of direction is possible at any time. There is no finality. Everything is kept in limbo [*in der Schwebe*]. The form of movement in the internet space is not a walking, striding or marching, but surfing or browsing (originally meaning 'to graze' or, metaphorically, 'to dip into a book'). These forms of movement are not linked to a direction; they also do not know of any fixed *paths*.

The internet space does not consist of phases of continuity and transition, but of discontinuous events or facts. Thus, no progress or development takes place in it. It is an ahistorical space. The time of internet space is a discontinuous and point-like Now-time. You move from one link to the next, from one Now to another. The Now does not possess duration. Nothing encourages you to linger for long on a particular Now-spot. Due to the numerous possibilities and alternatives there is no compulsion, no necessity to linger at a particular place. Prolonged lingering would only produce boredom.

The end of the linear constitution of the world not only results in loss. It also makes possible new forms of being and perceiving. Progressing gives way to hovering [*Schweben*]. Our perception becomes sensitized to non-causal relations. The end of that narrative linearity, whose strict selectivity forces events on to a narrow path, makes it necessary to find orientation, and to be able to move, amidst a high density of events. The arts and music of today also reflect this new form of perception. Aesthetic tension is not created by a narrative development, but by the superimposition and compression of events.

When intervals become shorter, the rate of succession of events accelerates. The compression of events, information and images makes it impossible to *linger*. The furious pace with which successive images pass does not permit any lingering contemplation. The images only fleetingly touch the retina, and do not attract lasting attention. Quickly they eject their visual stimulus and fade away. In contrast to knowledge

40

and experience [*Erfahrung*] in the emphatic sense, information and experienced events [*Erlebnisse*] produce no lasting or deep effects. The notions of truth and knowledge, by now, sound archaic. They rest on duration. Truth must endure. But, in fact, it fades away in the face of an increasingly shorter present. And knowledge is made possible by a temporal gathering which enframes the present with past and future. Such extended time characterizes truth as well as knowledge.

The production of technological or digital products is also subject to ever-shorter intervals. They age very quickly these days. The continual invention of newer versions and models means that they are short-lived. The compulsion towards the new shortens product life cycles. This compulsion is probably caused by the fact that nothing is able to produce duration. There is no *work*, no completion, but only continually new versions and variations. Even *design*, as a pure play with forms, and even 'pure' beauty in the Kantian sense – i.e. the semblance of beauty without any deep meaning, without involvement of anything extra-sensory, which merely causes 'pleasure' – require, on the basis of their definitions alone, permanent change, which is meant to serve the purpose of enlivening the mind, in other words, holding the attention. No meaning bestows duration on the semblance of beauty. No meaning *comports* [*verhält*] time.

The shrinkage of the present does not render it empty or thin it out. The paradox, rather, is that *everything* makes up the present at the same time, that everything has the opportunity, even *must* have the opportunity, of becoming part of the present. The present shortens and loses all duration; its time-frame diminishes more and more. At the same time, everything pushes into the present. The consequence is a pushing and shoving of images, events and information, which makes any lingering contemplation impossible. Thus, one zaps through the world.

41

6

Fragrant Crystal of Time

Even in broadest daylight, time moves
quietly like a thief in the night.

To stare at time, shout in its face,
until it startles and stops –
salvation or catastrophe?

Proust's narrative temporal technique may be interpreted as a
reaction against the 'age of haste' (*une époque de hâte*) in which
art itself is 'brief' (*bref*).[1] Art loses its epic breath. A general
shortness of breath befalls the world. For Proust, the age of
haste is the age of the railway, which, according to him, kills
all 'contemplation'.[2] Proust's critique of time also aims at
'cinematographic' time, which makes reality disintegrate into
a quick succession of images. His temporal strategy, directed
against the age of haste, consists in helping time to acquire
duration again, to return its scent to it.

Proust's search for lost time is a reaction against the progressive de-temporalization of existence [*Dasein*] which disintegrates the latter. The self disintegrates into a 'succession of moments' (*succession de moments*).[3] Thus, it loses all stability, all permanence.[4] The 'man that I was', Proust writes, 'no longer exists, I am another person' (*je suis un autre*).[5] Proust's novel about time, *In Search of Lost Time*, is an attempt to stabilize the identity of the self, which threatens to disintegrate. The temporal crisis is experienced as an identity crisis.

The key experience in the novel, as is well known, is the scent, the taste,[6] of the madeleine soaked in lime blossom tea. An intense feeling of happiness runs through Marcel when he brings a spoonful of tea with a little soaked piece of madeleine to his lips:

> An exquisite pleasure had invaded my senses, something isolated, detached, with no suggestion of its origin. And at once the vicissitudes of life had become indifferent to me, its disasters innocuous, its brevity illusory – this new sensation having had the effect, which love has, of filling me with a precious essence; or rather this essence was not in me, it *was* me. I had ceased now to feel mediocre, contingent, mortal.[7]

A small 'fragment of time in the pure state' (*un peu de temps à l'état pur*) is afforded Marcel.[8] This fragrant essence of time triggers a feeling of duration; thus he feels entirely freed from the 'vicissitudes of time' (*contingences du temps*). A temporal alchemy connects sensations and memories in a *crystal of time* which is outside of the past as well as the present.[9] Proust himself actually speaks of a fragrant crystal (*cristal*), a 'crystalline succession . . . of your silent, sonorous, fragrant, limpid hours' (*heures silencieuses, sonores, odorantes et limpides*).[10] Time is compressed into 'sealed vessels (*vases clos*), each one of them filled with things of a colour, a scent, and a temperature that are absolutely different one from another' (*dont chacun serait*

43

rempli de choses d'une couleur, d'une odeur, d'une température absolument différentes).[11] Although this 'vase full of scents' (*un vase rempli de parfums*)[12] is an 'extra-temporal' (*extra-temporel*) place to the extent that in it nothing elapses or is subject to temporal disintegration, it is nevertheless not supported by a timeless transcendence. The fragrant 'celestial nourishment' (*la céleste nourriture*)[13] is made up of *temporal* ingredients. Its scent is not that of a timeless eternity. Proust's strategy of duration releases the scent of *time*. It presupposes an historical existence; it presupposes that one has a *curriculum* vitae. Its scent is a scent of *immanence*.

Interestingly, the enchanting scent of time develops through the real scent. Apparently, the sense of smell is an organ of remembrance and reawakening. Although a *'mémoire involontaire'* [involuntary memory] may also be caused by tactile experiences (such as the stiffness of starched napkins or the sensation caused by uneven cobblestones), by acoustic ones (such as the sound a spoon makes on a plate), or visual ones (such as the view of the steeples of Martinsville), it is especially the recollection triggered by the smell and taste of the tea which exudes a particularly intense scent of time. It resurrects the world of childhood in its entirety.

It seems that scents and tastes reach deep into the past, touch on vast spaces of time. In this way, they form a scaffold holding the earliest memories. A single fragrance resurrects a childhood universe which was believed to have been lost:

> And as in the game wherein the Japanese amuse themselves by filling a porcelain bowl with water and steeping in it little pieces of paper which until then are without character or form, but, the moment they become wet, stretch and twist and take on colour and distinctive shape, become flowers or houses or people, solid and recognisable, so in that moment

all the flowers in our garden and in M. Swann's park, and the water-lilies on the Vivonne and the good folk of the village and their little dwellings and the parish church and the whole of Combray and its surroundings, taking shape and solidity, sprang into being, town and gardens alike, from my cup of tea.[14]

A 'tiny and almost impalpable drop' of tea covers such an expanse that a 'vast structure of recollection' finds room in it.[15] Taste (*le goût*) and smell (*l'odeur*) survive the demise of the personage and the decline of objects. They are islands of duration within the current of time that takes everything with it:

> But when from a long-distant past nothing subsists, after the people are dead, after the things are broken and scattered, taste and smell alone, more fragile but more enduring, more immaterial, more persistent, more faithful, remain poised a long time, like souls, remembering, waiting, hoping, amid the ruins of all the rest.[16]

In his *Understanding Media*, Marshall McLuhan refers to an interesting experiment which seems to provide a physiological basis, so to speak, for Proust's experience of the madeleine. The stimulation of brain tissue during surgery revives many memories, and these are saturated with special scents and smells which structure them into units and thus form a scaffold for early experiences.[17] Scent is steeped in history, so to speak. It is filled with stories, with narrative images. The sense of smell, as McLuhan remarks, is 'iconic'.[18] We might also say that it is the epic–narrative sense, connecting, interweaving, compressing temporal events into an image, a narrative form. Scents, which are steeped in images and history, are able to stabilize a self that is threatened with dissociation by providing it with a framing identity, an image of self. A stretch of time allows the self to come back to itself. This *return-to-self* is blissful [*beglückend*]. Where there are scents, there is *self*-gathering. [Wo es duftet, sammelt es *sich*.]

A scent is slow. Thus, as a medium, it is not adapted to the age of haste. Scents cannot be presented in as fast a sequence as optical images. In contrast to the latter, they can also not be accelerated. A society dominated by scents would probably also not develop any inclinations towards change or acceleration. It would live off its recollections and its memory, off those things that are slow and long-lasting. The age of haste, by contrast, is a 'cinematographic' age, one that is to a large extent shaped by the *visual*. Such an age accelerates the world into a 'cinematograph film of . . . things'.[19] Time disintegrates into a mere sequence of present moments. The age of haste is an age without scents. The scent of time is a manifestation of duration. Thus, it escapes 'activity' (*l'action*) and 'immediate enjoyment' (*la jouissance immediate*).[20] Scent is indirect, takes detours, and is mediated.

Proust's narrative temporal technique opposes temporal dissociation by framing events, uniting them into a coherent whole, or structuring them into certain periods. They are re-associated. A net of relations between events lets life appear liberated from sheer contingency and bestows significance on it. Proust is apparently convinced that in its depth life represents a densely woven net of connected events, and

> that life is perpetually weaving fresh threads which link one individual and one event to another, and that these threads are crossed and recrossed, doubled and redoubled to thicken the web, so that between any slightest point of our past and all the others a rich network of memories gives us an almost infinite variety of communicating paths to choose from.[21]

Proust opposes the incoherence of point-like presences, into which time threatens to disintegrate, with a temporal texture of references and similarities. As soon as one looks deeper into being one recognizes that all things are interconnected, that even the least of them communicates with a whole world. But the age of haste does not have the time to heighten perception. Only in the depth of being does a space open in which all things lie close to one another and communicate with one another. It is just this friendliness of being which gives the world its scent.

Truth also consists of relationships between events. Truth occurs when things communicate with each other on the basis of a similarity or some other form of closeness between them, when they turn towards each other and enter into relationships with each other, even befriend each other:

> truth [*la vérité*] will be attained by him [the author] only when he takes two different objects, states the connection between them . . . and encloses them in the necessary links of a well-wrought style; truth – and life too – can be attained by us only when, by comparing a quality common to two sensations, we succeed in extracting their common essence and in reuniting them to each other, liberated from the contingencies of time, within a metaphor[, thus linking them to each other through the ineffable efficacy of the combination of words].[22]

Only relationships based on similarity, friendship or affinity make things *true*. Truth is opposed to the accident of pure contiguity. Truth means *commitment, relationship* and *closeness*. Only through intense relationships do things become real in the first place:

> what we call reality is a certain connection between these immediate sensations and the memories which envelop us

simultaneously with them – a connection that is suppressed in a simply cinematographic vision . . . a unique connection which the writer has to rediscover in order to link forever in his phrase the two sets of phenomena which reality joins together.[23]

The formation of metaphors is also a practice concerning truth to the extent that it creates a network of relationships, and lays open the connecting paths and channels of communication between things. The formation of metaphor counteracts the atomization of being. And it is a temporal practice to the extent that it opposes the quick succession of isolated events with the duration, even fidelity, of a relationship. Metaphors are the scent of things which they release when they befriend each other.

'Immediate enjoyment' is not capable of experiencing beauty because the beauty of a thing appears 'only much later', in the light of another thing, or even through the significance of a reminiscence. Beauty is owed to duration, to a contemplative synopsis. It is not a momentous brilliance or attraction, but an afterglow, a phosphorescence of things. The 'cinematograph film of . . . things' does not have the temporality of beauty. The age of haste, its cinematographic succession of point-like presences, has no access to beauty or to truth. Only in lingering contemplation, even an ascetic restraint, do things unveil their beauty, their fragrant essence. It consists of temporal sedimentations emitting a phosphorescent glow.

7

The Time of the Angel

Who, if I cried out, would hear me among the angels'
Hierarchies? and even if one of them pressed me
suddenly against his heart: I would be consumed
in that overwhelming existence. For beauty is nothing
but the beginning of terror, which we still are just able to
    endure . . .
Every angel is terrifying.

Rainer Maria Rilke[1]

The oft-invoked end of the grand narrative is the end of epic
time, the end of the story as *intrigue*, which forces events on
to a narrative path and thus *conceives* a connection, a significance. The end of narration is in the first place a temporal
crisis. It destroys that temporal gravitation which gathers the
past and future into the present. If temporal gathering fails to
take place, time disintegrates. Postmodernity does not coin-
cide with a naïve and jubilatory affirmation of the end of
narrative time. Rather, the representatives of postmodernity

construct different temporal strategies and strategies of being [*Seinsstrategien*] which counteract the decay of time, counteract de-temporalization. Derrida's messianism also restores temporal gravitation without falling back into the old pattern of narration and identity. Derrida himself would not dispute that human life always requires a *construction*. Narration is not the only possible way of constructing biographical time.

The end of recounting does not necessarily reduce life to a mere counting. A deep layer of being, even *being* itself, can only reveal itself outside of recounting, that is, outside of *intrigue*, which aims for meaning and conception [*Ersinnen*]. Heidegger's turn to being was also a consequence of the narrative crisis. Apart from that, recounting and counting are not fundamentally different: recounting is a particular mode of counting. It creates suspense, which loads the sequence of events with meaning. Beyond a mere counting, it links events into a story. But *being* is not exhausted by number and counting, with numbering and recounting.

In the face of the crisis of *meaning*, Lyotard also took a turn towards *being*, turning the meaninglessness of narration into a particular experience of being. The difference between meaning and being forms an *ontological difference*. In the age characterized by narration and history, being retreats into the background in favour of meaning. But when meaning retreats in the course of de-narrativization, being announces itself. During such times, events no longer point towards their narrative meaning, towards their *What*, but towards their *That*. For Lyotard, *that something happens* is not just a fact. Rather, it points towards the occurrence of being [*Seinsgeschehen*] itself. This turn towards being brings Lyotard into proximity with Heidegger. Lyotard even expects an 'intensification of being' (*l'accroisement d'être*) from the end of narration.[2]

The end of narration has a temporal consequence. It ends linear time. Events are no longer linked up into stories. The narrative chain, which yields a meaning, operates by making a selection. It strictly regulates the sequence of events. An entirely random co-presence of sentences does not yield a meaning or a story. Thus, a narrative chain lets those things disappear which do not belong to its narrative system. In a certain sense, narration is blind, because it only looks in one direction. It therefore always has a blind spot.

The dissolution of the narrative chain throws time off its linear course, but the decay of linear–narrative time does not necessarily represent a catastrophe. Lyotard also sees in it a chance for liberation, as it frees perception from the *chains* of narration, from narrative coercion. Perception begins to hover, keeps itself suspended (*suspens*), and in this way becomes open to events that are free of narrative constraints, to events in the proper sense of the term. Things that would not find a place on the paths of narration, and would simply not be existent on them, become available to perception. The hovering is accompanied by the 'pleasure in welcoming the unknown'.[3]

At the beginning of his essay 'Newman: The Instant', Lyotard puts the words 'The Angel' as a short motto.[4] By setting 'angel' and 'instant' [*Augenblick*] so mysteriously close to each other, Lyotard embarks on a mystification of time. According to him, the end of narration does not deprive time of all gravitation. Rather, it releases the 'moment'. The moment is not the result of decay, not a temporal particle which remains after the dissolution of linear time. While it lacks *profound meaning*, it does possess *profoundness of being*. But its profoundness only concerns the pure presence of the *There*. The moment does not re-present. It only is a reminder 'that "there is", even before that which is has any significa-tion'.[5] The *There* is all it contains. Lyotard's angel makes no pronouncements; it has nothing to communicate. It shines in its pure presence.

51

Time deepens vertically instead of stretching along the horizontal narrative path. Narrative time is a continuous time. One event, by itself, announces the next event. Events follow each other and yield a meaning. But now, this temporal continuity stops, and a discontinuous, rugged time emerges. Events no longer contain any references to an ongoing process, to events following after them. An event now promises nothing beyond its instantaneous presence. A time without recollections and expectations emerges whose entire content is exhausted by a naked *There*.

Lyotard quotes Barnett Newman: 'My paintings are concerned neither with the manipulation of space nor with the image, but with the sensation of time.'[6] The *sensation* of time (*sensation de temps*) is not a *consciousness* of time. It lacks the temporal extension that is achieved by the constitutive work of consciousness. The sensation of time takes place *before* the synthesis of consciousness. The time in question is not one which *signifies*, but one which *affects*. For an instant, it rises like an 'affective cloud' in order to disappear into nothingness.[7] An event is not a *theme* to which consciousness could relate, but a *trauma* which cannot be captured by consciousness, which is entirely outside its control or annuls it.

Lyotard's response to the decay of *meaning*-ful time is not the usual nihilism, but an *animism* of a particular kind. Primary sense perception does not have a content that could be taken as a theme by consciousness; rather, it awakens the soul to life. It wrests the soul away from death, from the lethargy into which it would fall if it were not animated by it:

> The *anima* exists only as affected. Sensation, whether likeable or detestable, also announces to the anima that it would not even be, that it would remain inanimate, had nothing affected it. This soul is but the awakening of an affectability, and this remains disaffected in the absence of a timbre, a

52

color, a fragrance, in the absence of the sensible event that
excites it.[8]

The soul which is awakened into existence by primary sensations is an *anima minima*, a soul without a *mind*, which
communicates with *matter*, a soul without continuity or
memory which altogether evades a psychoanalytic, or any
other hermeneutic, understanding.

According to Lyotard, after the end of narration, all content is also evacuated from the arts, and art becomes an art of
pure presence. It rests solely on 'the vow the soul makes for
escaping the death'.[9] Sounds, colours and voices are emptied
of the meanings which culture attaches to them. Deprived
of cultural significance, art must direct attention to its character as an event. Its task consists in bearing witness to the
fact that something *takes place*: 'The *aistheton* is an event; the
soul exists only if that event stimulates it; when it is lacking,
the soul is dissipated into the nothingness of the inanimate.
Works of art are charged with honouring this miraculous
and precarious condition.'[10] The soul owes its existence to
the *aistheton*, the sensual event. Without the *aistheton*, there
would only be anaesthesia. Aesthetics is a recipe against
anaesthesia.

Lyotard is of the opinion that it is precisely the end of
narrative time which makes it possible to come close to the
'mystery of being',[11] that it leads to an 'intensification of
being'.[12] But he goes too far in marginalizing the nihilis-
tic dimension in this. The decay of the temporal continuum
renders existence radically fragile. The soul is permanently
exposed to the danger of death and the terror of nothingness,
because the event which wrests it from death lacks any duration. The intervals between events are death zones. During
these eventless in-between times, the soul falls into lethargy.
The joy of being mingles with a fear of death. Exaltation

53

is followed by depression, by an ontological depression even.

The profundity of being is at the same time its absolute poverty. It altogether lacks the *space for dwelling*. In this respect, Lyotard differs radically from Heidegger. Lyotard's mystery of being concerns a pure being-*There* [*Da*-sein]. The 'anima minima' which participates in the mystery of being is ultimately the soul of the simplest monad, of that vegetative soul which has no consciousness and no mind. It knows only two states: horror and euphoria, the terror of the threat of death and the relief or joy over having escaped it after all. One should not even speak of joy, because joy is an achievement of consciousness. Lyotard's rugged, discontinuous event-time on the edge of the abyss of time is not a time for living or dwelling. Living is more than vegetating, more than merely being awake. The end of narrative time does not necessarily have to lead to a vegetative time. There is a time for living which is neither narrative, nor vegetative – a time that is situated beyond themes and traumas.

8

Fragrant Clock

A Short Excursus on Ancient China

Flowers, red, protrude out of the vase
Incense rises in spirals.
Neither questions nor answers,
the *Ruyi*[1] careless on the floor.
Dian let the tone of his zither fade,
Zhao abstained from plucking the strings:
In all this, there is a melody,
which you may sing and to which you may dance.

Du Dongpo[2]

In China, an incense clock called *hsiang yin* (literally: seal of fragrance) was in use until the end of the nineteenth century. Until the mid-twentieth century, Europeans believed it simply to be a censer; the idea of measuring time with incense was obviously alien to them, as perhaps was the idea that time could take the form of a fragrance.[3] The clock was called 'seal of fragrance' because the part where the incense was burned had the shape of a seal. Tso Kuei describes such a seal of fragrance as follows: 'Engraved into wood, patterns in the form of seal script characters are revealed when the incense in them is burned at drinking parties or before images of Buddha.'⁴ The incense seal is a figure with one wick running through it so that the glow may move along the whole length of it. A template, which often includes written characters, is filled with pulverized incense. When it is lifted, a typeface made of incense emerges. It either consists of a single sign, often *fu* (luck), or of several signs which, together, sometimes form a *kŏan*.⁵ *How many lives before I obtain my flowers*, reads a mysterious *kŏan* on one of these incense seals.⁶ In the middle of the seal, the words 'my flowers' are replaced by the image of a flower. The seal itself has the shape of the flower of a plum tree. The glow of the incense traces, so to speak, the flower-*kŏan* by moving, sign by sign, through the whole seal, that is, by burning it down.

Hsiang yin is the name of the whole incense clock, which consists of several parts. The incense seal of fragrance burns in an ornate box and is protected against draughts by a lid whose openings also are shaped in the form of characters or other symbols. Often, philosophical or poetic writings are engraved on the box. The whole clock, then, is surrounded by fragrant words and images. The rich meaning of the engraved verses already radiates a scent. A *hsiang yin* with a flower-shaped opening in the lid bears the following poem on one of its sides:

> You see the flowers
> You listen to the bamboo
> And your heart will be at peace.
> Your problems will be cleared away.
> The ground burns
> Fragrant music
> You will have . . .⁷

As a medium for measuring time, incense differs in many respects from water or sand. Fragrant time does not flow or trickle away. Nothing is emptied. Rather, the scent of the incense fills the room, even turns time into space; it thus gives it a semblance of duration. Although the glow permanently transforms the incense into ash, the ash does not disintegrate into dust. Rather, it retains the shape of the writing. The incense seal therefore loses none of its meaning even after having turned into ash. The transience which may be evoked by the inexorable progression of the glowing incense gives way to a feeling of duration.

A *hsiang yin* really exudes a scent. The fragrance of incense intensifies the scent of time. This is what makes this clock so refined. A *hsiang yin* tells the hour through the fragrant fluidity of time, which neither flows nor trickles away.

> I sit at peace – burning an incense seal,
> Which fills the room with scent of pine and cedar.
> When all the burning stops, a clear image is seen,
> Of the green moss upon the epigraph's carved words.[8]

The incense fills the room with the scent of pine and cedar. The fragrant room is soothing, and sets the poet's mind at rest. The ash is not a reminder of transience; it is 'green moss' which even highlights the writing. Time *stands still* within the scent of pine and cedar. It comes to rest, so to speak, within the 'clear image'. Framed within a figure, it does not trickle away. It is held, even arrested, within the scent, in the scent's hesitant whiling. The puffs of smoke rising from the incense are also perceived as figures. Ting Yün writes:

> Butterflies appear as if in a dream,
> Twisting and reeling about like dragons,

Like birds, like the phoenix,
Like worms in spring, like snakes in the fall.[9]

The plethora of figures makes time congeal as if it were a painting. *Time becomes space*. The spatial side-by-side of spring and autumn also arrests time. What emerges is a *still life of time*.

To the poet Ch'iao Chi, the smoke of the *hsiang yin* appears as an old writing which gives him a deep feeling of duration.

Like billowing silks, sinuous, cloud-tipped
Smoke has written ancient script,
From the last of the incense ash to burn.
There lingered warmth in my precious urn,
While moonlight had already died
In the garden pool outside.[10]

This is a poem addressed to duration. While the moonlight in the garden pond has long since faded away, the ash is not yet completely cold. The censer still radiates warmth. The warmth persists. This hesitant whiling delights the poet.

The Chinese poet Hsieh Chin (*c.*1260–1368) writes about the rising smoke of the incense seal:

Smoke from an incense seal marks the passing
Of a fragrant afternoon.[11]

The poet does not lament that a beautiful afternoon has passed, because every time has a scent proper to it. Why should one lament the passing of an afternoon? The scent of the afternoon will be followed by the pleasant smell of the evening. And night, too, exudes its own fragrance. These scents of time are not narrative, but contemplative. They are not arranged into a sequence. Rather, they rest in themselves.

58

Hundreds of flowers in spring, the moon in autumn,
A cool breeze in summer, and snow in winter;
If there is no vain cloud in your mind
For you it is a good season.[12]

The good time is accessible for a mind that has *emptied* itself of all things 'useless'. It is particularly the *emptiness* of mind, freeing it from desire, which deepens time. This depth connects every point in time with *all of being*, with its fragrant intransience. It is desire itself which makes time radically transient by causing the mind to rush ahead [*fortstürzen*]. Where it stands *still*, where it rests in itself, there occurs the *good time*.

9

The Round Dance of the World

Scent of the pine trees –
A lizard scurries
Across the hot stone.

In 1927, *Le Temps retrouvé* [*Time Regained*] was published in Paris. The same year saw the publication of Heidegger's *Being and Time* in Germany. There are numerous similarities between these two works, which, at first glance, seem so different. Like Proust's project on time, *Being and Time* sets itself against the increasing disintegration of human existence, against the decay of time into a mere sequence of point-like presences. Contrary to Heidegger's aspiration that *Being and Time* represent a phenomenology of human existence of timeless validity, his work is in reality a product of *its* time. Historically specific processes and time-independent characteristics of human existence are intermingled in it. Thus, Heidegger offers a problematic explanation of the 'destruction of the everyday world'[1] through acceleration, which he says is the result of a 'tendency towards nearness' that is intrinsic to *Dasein*'s essence:

> Dasein is essentially de-distancing. As the being that it is, it lets beings be encountered in nearness . . . *An essential tendency towards nearness lies in Dasein*. All kinds of increasing speed which we are more or less compelled to go along with today push for overcoming distance. With the 'radio', for example, Dasein is bringing about today a de-distancing of the 'world', which is unforeseeable in its meaning for Dasein, by way of expanding and destroying the everyday surrounding world.[2]

To what extent is 'de-distancing' – as a mode of being of *Dasein*, which I use as a means for spatially opening up my surroundings – related to that unleashed acceleration which steers towards *the suspension of space itself*? Apparently, Heidegger does not realize that the age of the radiophonic, even the entire 'age of haste', is based on forces far greater than the 'tendency towards nearness' intrinsic to *Dasein*'s essence, and which make *Dasein*'s orientation in space possible in the first place. The total removal of space is something altogether different from that 'de-distancing' which affords *Dasein* a spatial existence.

The new media abolish space itself. Hyperlinks make pathways disappear. Electronic mail does not need to conquer mountains and oceans. Strictly speaking, it is no longer something 'ready-to-hand'. Instead of 'hands' it immediately reaches the eyes. The age of the new media is an age of implosion. Space and time implode into a here and now. Everything is subject to de-distancing. There are no longer any sacred spaces which one may not 'de-distance', i.e. spaces whose being set aside [*Ausgespartsein*] is part of their essence. Spaces with a scent *hold* their appearance *in reserve* [*sparen ihr Erscheinen*]. An auratic distance is inherent in them. The contemplative, lingering gaze is not de-distancing. In his later writings, Heidegger himself turned against the unlimited de-distancing of the world. Thus, origin is something which 'halts in its withdrawal, and holds itself in reserve'.[3] It does not exhaust or divest itself. According to Heidegger, the 'nearness to the origin is a nearness which still holds something back in reserve' [*sparende Nähe*].[4]

The 'they', which Heidegger generalizes into an ontological constant, is in reality a phenomenon of *his* time. It is, in a manner of speaking, a contemporary of Heidegger's. Thus, the temporal experience of the 'they' corresponds exactly to the 'cinematographic' time which, according to Proust, characterizes the 'age of haste'. Time is dispersed into a mere sequence of point-like presences. The 'they' 'is so little interested in the "matter in question" that, as soon as it catches sight of it, it already is looking for the next thing'.[5] The 'they' zaps through the world. Thus, Heidegger speaks of a 'dispersed non-lingering' and of a *'never dwelling anywhere'* [*Aufenthaltslosigkeit*].[6]

Heidegger realized early on that the emptiness of being goes hand in hand with the acceleration of life. In his lecture course of 1929/30, he says:

Why do we find no meaning for ourselves any more, i.e. no essential possibility of being? Is it because an *indifference* yawns at us out of all things, an indifference whose grounds we do not know? Yet who can speak in such a way when world trade, technology, and the economy seize hold of man and keep him moving?[7]

Heidegger explains the general haste in terms of the inability to perceive silence, the long-lasting and slowness. Where there is no duration, acceleration, in the sense of a purely quantitative intensification, sets in, in order to compensate for the lack of duration, even for the lack of being:

Acceleration [Die *Schnelligkeit*] . . . not-being-able-to-bear the stillness of hidden growth . . . purely quantitative enhancement, blindness to what is truly momentary, which is not fleeting but opens up eternity.[8]

Heidegger's philosophy of time is connected to *his* times. Thus, his critical comments regarding time, for instance about the permanent shortage of time, are also aimed at *his* times:

Why do we have no time? To what extent do we not wish to lose any time? Because we need it and wish to use it. For what? For our everyday occupations, to which we have long since become enslaved. . . .This *not having any time* is ultimately a *greater being lost of the self* than that wasting time which leaves itself time.[9]

Heidegger invokes 'what is essential in Dasein' and what 'cannot be forcibly brought about by any busyness or mad rush'.[10] 'Essential existence' is 'slow'. Heidegger explicitly turns against the 'modern', which is characterized by point-like presences and discontinuity.[11] As a characteristic manifestation of modernity, the 'they' only perceives the narrow tip of the actual. Thus, it rushes from one presence to the next.

The decay of time also takes hold of the identity of *Dasein*. *Dasein* is 'dispersed in the multiplicity of what "happens" daily'.[12] It is 'lost in the making present of the today',[13] and thus loses the continuity of its self. The age of haste is an age of 'dispersion'. This awakens the need 'to pull itself together [*Zusammenholen*] from the dispersion and the disconnectedness'.[14] But narrative identity only establishes a connection, while Heidegger's strategy regarding the question of identity is to aim for the extraction of 'the primordial stretching along of the whole of existence, which is not lost and does not need a connection', namely 'a *steadiness that has been stretched along* – the steadiness in which Da-sein as fate "incorporates" into its existence birth and death and their "between"'.[15] This 'fatefully whole[,] stretching',[16] namely *history*, is more than a story which establishes a connection. It is not a narratively constructed picture, but a pre-narrative framing which encloses 'birth and death and their "between"'. *Dasein* assures itself of itself independently of a narrative construction of identity. Heidegger's strategy regarding time and identity is a response to the narrative crisis of his times. The strategy formulates a notion of identity which would still be viable in an age of general de-narrativization.

Being and Time is based on an insight that is specific to its times, that the loss of historical meaningfulness leads to the decay of time into an accelerating sequence of isolated events, that because of a lack of gravitation or an anchoring in meaning time rushes off without hold or aim. Heidegger's strategy regarding time consists in a re-anchoring of time; in giving it significance, a new hold; in enframing it again within a historical line [*Zug*], so that it does not disperse into a meaningless, accelerating succession of events. Against the threatened end of history, Heidegger emphatically invokes history itself. However, he knows very well that the gravitation, the historical meaningfulness which is meant to set time right again, cannot be of a theological or teleological kind, and he therefore opts for an existential concept of history instead. The historical traction now originates from the emphasis on the self. Heidegger concentrates time by integrating the temporal horizons by way of their relation to the self. History as *directed* time protects time against decay, against its dispersion into a pure sequence of point-like presences. In this, it is the self that provides the direction. The '*constancy* of the self', this essence of authentic historicity, is duration, which does not pass. It does not elapse. The one who exists authentically has time always, so to speak. He or she always has time because time is *self*, and does not lose time because of not losing *him- or herself*:

> Just as the person who exists inauthentically constantly loses time and never 'has' any, it is the distinction of the temporality of authentic existence that in resoluteness it never loses time and 'always has time'.[17]

The shortage of time, on the contrary, is a symptom of inauthentic existence. *Dasein* in its inauthentic existence loses its time because it loses *itself* to the world: 'Busily losing himself in what is taken care of, the irresolute person loses his time in them, too. Hence, his characteristic way of talking: "I have no time".'[18] Ultimately, Heidegger's strategy regarding time consists in transforming 'I have no time' into 'I always have time.' It is a strategy based on duration, an attempt at regaining the lost *mastery of time* through an existential mobilization of the self.

In his later writings, Heidegger moves further and further away from the historical model of time. The place of history is taken by the seasons or other figures of repetition:

> In the pathway's seasonally changing breeze this knowing gladsomeness ... thrives ... Along its trail winter's storm encounters harvest's day, the agile excitation of Spring and the serene dying of Autumn meet, the child's game and the elder's wisdom gaze at each other. And in a unique harmony, whose echo the pathway carries with it silently *here and there*, everything is made *gladsome*.[19]

The 'silent harmony' of the seasons and its echo, which continues, even renews itself in the '*here and there*', suggest duration. The world is an acoustic space with its own natural oscillation, in which nothing fades away or elapses. The 'gathering play' which surrenders nothing to disappearance or dispersion creates a fulfilled duration:

> In the coolness of the autumn day, the fire of summer finishes in cheerful serenity . . . The cheerful serenity of the autumn coolness, which harbors the summer within itself, drifts about this country path every year with its gathering play.[20]

Again and again, Heidegger uses the trope of the 'back and forth'[21] as a counter-trope to historical time. In the movement of the back-and-forth, time comes to stand still [*zum Stehen*], so to speak. A duration a-*rises* [ent-*steht*]. Heidegger's poem 'Time' goes:

> How far?
> Only when it stops, the clock,
> with its pendulum swinging back and forth,
> only then do you hear: it goes and is gone and goes
> no more.
> Already late in the day, the clock,
> only a faint track toward time,
> which, near finitude,
> a-rises from it.[22]

The 'back and forth' produces duration within cyclical change. Heidegger's *Pathway* is itself constructed like a pendulum clock. The text sets out with the words: 'It runs from the park gate towards Ehnried'. And towards the end of the text, we read: 'From Ehnried the way turns back to the park gate.'[23] The back-and-forth of its course makes the pathway a figure of repetition and gathering. Nothing progresses without returning. All *Forth* is caught by a *Back*, as if by an echo. This back-and-forth is also reflected in the play of children:

> Out of the oak's bark the boys carved their boats: equipped with rudder and tiller they floated in Metten brook or in the school fountain. The world-wide journeys of these games reached their *destination* [*Ziel*] easily and found their way *back* to shore again.[24]

Nothing is lost to indeterminacy. And nothing is subject to change. The country path is a silent place of eternal repetition. Everything remains gathered: 'The pathway gathers in whatever has its coming-to-presence [*sein Wesen*] along the way; to all who pass this way it gives what is theirs.'[25] Everything rests in the timelessly valid 'coming-to-presence', in an eternal presence. The pathway's back-and-forth silences the world into the 'Same'. In the pendulum strokes of its back-and-forth, the world a-*rises*. The pathway represents a clearly delineated world of duration with its own natural oscillation. Everything stands within the simple lustre of a perspicuous order. Nothing escapes the eye and hand of the mother: 'The eye and hand of the mother surrounded their world [i.e. that of all things]. It was as if her unspoken care protected all that came to be [*alles Wesen*].'[26]

The country path does not strive towards a *goal* [*Ziel*]. Rather, it rests in itself in contemplative fashion. It illustrates a *via contemplativa*. The back-and-forth frees it from having a goal without exposing it to destructive dispersion. A peculiar gathering is intrinsic to it. It does not follow a course towards ... but lingers. It silences the directed, spasmodic time of labour into duration. As a place for contemplative lingering, the path symbolizes a dwelling that does not need a goal or purpose, one that can do without a theology or teleology.

The world is a 'round dance' of 'earth and sky, divinities

and mortals'.[27] The 'round dance' is at the same time a temporal formula, an eternal circling in itself which prevents any spatio-temporal dispersion. Everything remains gathered in the 'ring' of the world, in the 'radiance of their [i.e. of the fourfold's] simple oneness'.[28] The 'sky', too, is a timeless circling in itself, an eternal up-and-down. It is the 'path of the sun, the course of the changing moon, the wandering glitter of the stars, the year's seasons and their changes, the light and dusk of day, the gloom and glow of night, the clemency and inclemency of weather, the drifting clouds and blue depth of the ether'.[29] At the temporal level, the strictly symmetrical structure of the world creates the impression of a time that stands still. The symmetry of the world, which suggests an immovable, uniform order, extends into language. Heidegger even emphasizes it with special figures of speech. His philosophy consists not only of arguments, but – problematically – also of verses. Types of syntax and rhyme patterns are intentionally employed to create, for instance, the feeling of an eternally valid order. Thus, the beautiful, symmetrical order of the world, the 'fouring', is invoked,[30] in a poem that is, not coincidentally, made up of two stanzas of *four* symmetrically composed lines. The 'radiance of their simple oneness'[30] is completed in the metrical radiance of 'mist diffuses/blessing muses' [*Regen rinnt/Segen sinnt*].

Forests spread
Brooks plunge
Rocks persist
Mist diffuses

Meadows wait
Springs well
Winds dwell
Blessing muses[31]

10

The Scent of Oak Wood

Why has no one ever invented a god of slowness?

Peter Handke

The acceleration of life in general robs the human being of the capacity for contemplation. Thus, those things which only reveal themselves in contemplative lingering remain hidden. Acceleration is not a primary process which only subsequently leads to a loss of the *vita contemplativa*. Rather, the relationship between acceleration and the loss of the *vita contemplativa* is a complex one. It is precisely the inability to linger in contemplation which creates the centrifugal forces which bring about a general haste and dispersion. Ultimately, the acceleration of life as well as the loss of the capacity for contemplation can be derived from a historical constellation in which the belief was lost that things exist of their own accord and remain eternally in their suchness [*So-Sein*]. A general de-facticization of the world takes away their individual radiance and degrades them into objects that can be produced. Devoid of spatial and temporal conditions, they can now be made and produced. Facticity gives way to production. Being is de-facticized into a process.

In modern technology, Heidegger recognizes the danger of the de-facticization of being into a process that can be regulated and planned. Heidegger's being is exactly the opposite of a process. A *procedere* implies continuous change. Being, by contrast, does not proceed. Rather, it oscillates within itself and remains within the 'Same'. This is also part of its facticity: 'The simple conserves the puzzle of what abides and what is great. Spontaneously it enters men and yet needs a lengthy growth. With the unpretentiousness of the ever Same it hides its blessing.'[1] A process proceeds towards a goal. The faster the goal is reached, the more efficient the process. Acceleration is inherent in purely functional processes. Thus, a processor which knows only of processes of calculation is subject to pressures of acceleration. It can be accelerated to any degree because it does not possess a meaningful structure, or a rhythm, of its own, because it can be reduced to nothing but a functional efficiency which registers any delay as a disturbance. A computer does not hesitate. The *work* of pure calculation is structured by a temporality that has no access to lingering. From the perspective of a *procedere*, lingering is nothing but a standstill that needs to be overcome as soon as possible. Rest is, at best, a pause which has no relevance for the efficiency of the work of calculation. Thus, Heidegger writes: '*Precipitance and surprise* [*Übereilung und Überraschung*] ... The former arises in calculation./The latter comes out of the unexpected./The former follows a plan./The latter visits a lingering.'[2]

Contemplative lingering presupposes things which last. It is not possible to linger for long on events or images which quickly succeed one another. Heidegger's 'thing' satisfies this condition of lasting. It is a place of duration. It is interesting that Heidegger also uses the verb 'to linger' [*verweilen*] transitively, giving it the sense of 'gathering'. The human being can linger on things because things *make* the world relations *linger*. The transitive lingering of the world makes possible the intransitive lingering on things: 'The thing things. In thinging, it stays [*verweilt*] earth and sky, divinities and mortals. Staying [*Verweilend*], the thing brings the four, in their remoteness, near to one another.'[3] The earth is 'the serving bearer, blossoming and fruiting, spreading out in rock and water, rising up into plant and animal'.[4] The sky is the 'path of the sun, the course of the changing moon, the wandering glitter of the stars, the year's seasons and their changes, the light and dusk of day, the gloom and glow of night, the clemency and inclemency of weather, the drifting clouds and blue depth of the ether'.[5] These eternally valid coordinates of the world, which are reflected in the things, are meant to lend human dwelling the 'slowness and constancy with which the tree grows'.[6] Heidegger's philosophy of autochthony and home [*Bodenständigkeit und Heimat*] tries to stabilize the ground on which the human abode rests, the very ground which has long since begun to shift, or even threatens to disappear altogether.

Heidegger's thing exists entirely outside of usage or consumption. It is a place for contemplative lingering. A jug serves Heidegger as an example of a thing which makes the abode [*Aufent*halt] in the world possible. It is certainly not a coincidence that Heidegger uses a jug as his example of a thing. For, a jug is a con*tainer*. It gives a *hold* [*Halt*] to its con*tent* [*In*halt], so that *nothing trickles or flows away*. It is these *specific* properties of a jug which Heidegger uses in order to demonstrate what a thing *as such* actually is.[7]

Heidegger defines 'dwelling' as a 'staying with things'.[8] He could also have said: 'lingering on things'. But the staying needs a hold:

More essential than constituting rules is that human beings find the way to their abode [*Aufenthalt*] in the truth of Being. This abode [*Aufenthalt*] first yields the experience of something we can hold on to. . . . 'Hold' in our language means 'protective heed' ['*Hut*']. Being is the protective heed that holds the human being in his ek-sistent essence to the truth of such protective heed . . .[9]

Without hold, the human being is adrift [*haltlos*] and without protection. Only a hold also *comports* [*verhält*] time, brings out what is durable [*das Haltbare*]. Without hold what occurs is the tearing away of time [*Fortriß der Zeit*], the bursting of the temporal dam. Without a hold it tears away. Ultimately, the acceleration derives from the groundlessness [*Haltlosigkeit*], the absence of abodes, the absence of holds. The accelerated sequences and succession of events as the form of movement of today's world are an expression of the missing hold. The general acceleration of the lifeworld is only a symptom whose cause lies deeper. Techniques of deceleration or relaxation cannot stop the tearing away of time. They do not remove the cause.

The world, in fact, consists for the most part of things and arrangements produced by human beings. Heidegger's world, by contrast, is always already given, even dictated [*vorgegeben*], prior to any human intervention. This anterior always-already constitutes its facticity. The world is a gift [*Gabe*] which evades all human grasp. It is a world of eternal repetition. While modern technology moves human beings further and further away from the ground, from the earth, and at the same time also frees them from the needs associated with it, Heidegger insists on 'autochthony'. He is sceptical towards any de-facticization, any form of producing the world, even though humanity ultimately owes its survival to the latter. Against a world that is de-facticized into a process that can be regulated and produced, Heidegger invokes the 'unproducable' or the 'mystery' [*das Geheimnis*].

Heidegger uses *conservatio* as a temporal strategy for creating duration. Human beings, he says, are 'hearers of the Origin' [*Hörige ihrer Herkunft*].[10] Only their 'distant origin' [*lange Herkunft*] gives them a 'home'. 'Old age' is 'wisdom'. Thus, Heidegger turns against the shrinking present which characterizes a modernity that does not pass on any traditions and in which everything very quickly becomes antiquated. 'Wisdom' rests on continuity and duration. In Heidegger's world, there is an unchanging order which is to be taken up, to be inherited and to be repeated. The compulsion to follow the new is set in opposition to the 'always same'.

Part of facticity is a passivity, which is expressed in formulations such as 'letting ourselves be concerned' [*sich-angehen-lassen*] and 'be thrown or called'. The passivity of 'be concerned' is opposed to *procedure* [*Vorgehen*]. Heidegger specifically uses the former as a means against the de-facticization of the world. Heidegger's thing also puts the human being into a passive mode, by making it something that is 'be-thinged'.[11] As someone be-thinged, the human being lingers with things. The thing is not a product that is subject to a production process. It gains an autonomy from, even an authority over, the human being. It represents the weightiness of the world, which the human being must take on and must comply with. Faced with the conditioning thing, the human being must renounce the wish to be elevated to the status of the unconditioned.

God represents the 'unproducable', which evades human intervention. He is the un-conditioned as such.[12] The de-facticization of the world renders it entirely godless. 'Meagre time' is a time without God. The human being has to remain someone be-thinged, a 'mortal'. The attempt to eliminate death would be sacrilege, a human 'machination'. It would ultimately equal the elimination of God. Heidegger remained a *homo doloris*, a thinker of pain. Only the *homo doloris* has access to the scent of the 'eternal'. Maybe Heidegger would say that the elimination of death would mean the end of the *anthropos*, and that, faced with immortality, the human being must re-invent itself.

Heidegger's 'being' has a temporal aspect: '"Whiling", "tarrying", "perpetuating", is ... the old sense of the word "being".'[13] Only being permits lingering, because it 'whiles' and 'perpetuates' [*weilt und währt*]. Thus, the age of haste and acceleration is an age of forgetfulness of being. 'The Pathway' always evokes duration and slowness: 'Behind the Schloss the tower of St. Martin's Church rises. Slowly, almost hesitatingly, eleven strokes of the hour sound in the night.'[14] Temporal figures such as 'hesitation', 'waiting' or 'patience'[15] have the purpose of founding a positive relationship with what escapes any readily available present. They do not indicate a condition of deprivation. Rather, they are characterized by a *More of the Less*. The waiting does not expect anything concrete. Rather, it refers to what evades any kind of calculation. Likewise, hesitation does not mean indecisiveness, but is a relationship with what eludes any determined grasping. It is the positive drawing 'toward what withdraws'.[16] It is animated by the 'slow shyness before the unproducable'. A thinker must patiently wait in this 'draft, this current' [*Zugwind dieses Zuges*], instead of 'seeking refuge from any draft too strong for them'.[17]

'Meagre time' is a time without scent. It lacks that which endures, that which creates stable bonds across large stretches of time. Heidegger makes extensive use of the terms 'slow' and 'slowly'. The 'ones to come' are the 'lingering [*langsamen*], long-hearing founders' of truth,[18] who, 'with the courage to go slowly'[19] and with the 'expectant decisiveness to be patient', trace the 'measured signs [*langsamen Zeichen*]

74

of the incalculable'.[20] The 'scent of oak wood', in particular, represents the scent of what endures and is slow. The scent of the 'eternal' drifts through the country path, the path that founds 'meaningfulness'. However, Heidegger's 'meaning' is a-teleological, even non-perspectival. It is not dominated by a goal or purpose that needs to be realized. It is without direction. It is not structured in a narrative or linear fashion. It is, so to speak, a *gyrating* meaning which deepens into being. Heidegger's thinking resolutely performs the turn from meaning to being. Only in the face of a goal does acceleration make sense. What does not have a direction, by contrast, what oscillates or is fulfilled within itself – in other words what does not contain any teleological moment and is no process – does not create any pressure to accelerate.

Heidegger's God guards the 'eternal', the 'puzzle of what abides and what is great'. Thrownness and facticity characterize the human being's relation to God. Any human 'machination' makes the human being more 'hard of hearing' for the language of God, which is drowned out by the 'noise of media [*Apparate*] which they [i.e. those of today] almost consider to be the voice of God'.[21] God seeks those moments of 'stillness' which emerge when the technical apparatuses are turned off and fall silent. The accelerating time of the apparatuses pulls the world and the things out of their own time. In the final instance, Heidegger's thought turns against the historical shift from repetition and reproduction towards manufacture and production, from thrownness and facticity towards freedom and self-affirmation. God is the instance which puts the seal of eternal validity on a meaningful and ordered structure. He stands for repetition and identity. After all, there is no God of change and difference. He stabilizes time, and acceleration, ultimately, is the consequence of the death of God. Every de-facticization of the world by human power leads to a de-temporalization. Only once the world is left alone in its own time, even stands *still*, Heidegger believes, does the 'message [*Zuspruch*] of the pathway'[22] become audible as the language of God. Only where the things rest again in the gravity of their 'old origin',[23] is God *God*. Through the world's and the things' own time, God reveals himself as the God of slowness, even as the God of home [*Heimat*].

There can be no doubt that the later Heidegger invokes the return of conditions of the archaic and pre-modern world through their romantic transfiguration, conditions whose overcoming has meant essential progress for mankind. But despite all the scepticism towards his theology of 'autochthony' and 'home', we should listen to what he has to say when he approaches what endures and what is slow. There are, indeed, events, forms and oscillations which are only open to a long, contemplative gaze, but remain hidden to the working gaze; things that are subtle, fleeting; inconspicuous things, minor things [*das Geringe*]; things that hover or retreat, which evade any violent efforts at their capture.

Heidegger is on his way towards another time, a time that is not the time of work,[24] but the time of the enduring and slow, which makes lingering possible. Work, ultimately, aims at domination and assimilation. It destroys the distance to things. The contemplative gaze, by contrast, *goes easy on* them, letting them be in their own space or radiance. This gaze is a practice characterized by friendliness. It is more than common-sense wisdom when Heidegger says: 'Abandonment does not take. Abandonment gives. It gives the inexhaustible power of the Simple.'[25] The contemplative gaze is ascetic in the sense that it renounces the removal of distance, renounces assimilation. This is a point at which Heidegger is close to Adorno: 'in the long, contemplative look . . . the urge towards the object is always deflected, reflected. Contemplation without violence, the source of all the joy of truth, presupposes that he who contemplates does not absorb the object into

76

himself'.[26] The long, contemplative gaze trains itself in the preservation of a distance to the things, without, though, losing their nearness. Its spatial formula is that of 'a distanced nearness'.[27]

11

Profound Boredom

When we forgot the current date:
Those were the times.
That was the time.
When the dreams came and went
one right after the other,
some leading us to hell's,
others to heaven's door:
Those were the times.
That was the time . . .

Peter Handke[1]

Right in the middle of the revolution, in the middle of escalating, dramatic events, Büchner's character Danton is overcome by profound boredom:

Camille: Hurry, Danton, we've no time to lose.
Danton [getting dressed]: But time is losing us. How boring
   life is: day after day we put on our shirts and pull up our

trousers, crawl into bed in the evening and out again in the morning, place one foot relentlessly in front of the other, with nothing to suggest things will ever be different.[2]

The time of revolution, whose subject is the individual resolutely taking action, is paradoxically struck by profound boredom. Apparently, the determination of the free subject to take action does not release the kind of intense binding energies that would allow for an experience of fulfilled time. Thus, Camille is longing for past times: 'The ordinary delusions that people call "sanity" are all so unbearably boring. The luckiest man of them all was the one that imagined he was God the father, God the son and God the Holy Ghost.'[3]

It is not an uneventful time in which profound boredom first arises. The historical time of the revolution, which is rich in events, but has fallen out of the condition of duration and repetition, is particularly susceptible to boredom. The tiniest repetition is perceived as monotony. Boredom is not the antithesis of resolute action; rather, they involve each other. The resolve to act decisively is precisely what deepens the boredom. Thus, in the midst of intense action, Danton, the revolutionary, feels left alone by time. The true shortage of time [*Zeitnot*] does not consist in the loss of time, but in the fact that 'time is losing us'. Time itself becomes vacuous. Or it is devoid of the gravitation that would bind and gather. The boredom, ultimately, derives from the *emptiness of time*. Time is no longer fulfilling. The freedom of the acting subject by itself does not produce any temporal gravitation. Where its impulse to act does not attach to a new object, an empty interval emerges, and this interval is boring. Fulfilled time does not have to be varied or full of events. It is a time of duration in which repetition is not perceived as such. Only after the decay of duration does repetition become topical

79

and problematic. Thus, any ordinary form of repetition torments Danton, the revolutionary.

In his lecture course of 1929/30, Heidegger asks about the fundamental attunement [*Grundstimmung*] which determines [*be*-stimmt] the present day, which 'pervades *us* fundamentally'.[4] To begin with, he thinks he can detect ardent efforts at a new self-determination. 'Today's man', he says, strives to find a role for himself, a meaning, a value. Heidegger views these excessive efforts at finding a meaning for man as a symptom of profound boredom: 'Why do we find no meaning for ourselves any more, i.e. no essential possibility of being? . . . *Do things ultimately stand in such a way with us that a profound boredom draws back and forth like a silent fog in the abysses of Dasein?*'[5] Heidegger interprets profound boredom as *the* sign of our times, and he derives it from 'beings' telling refusal of themselves as a whole'. This withdrawal [*Entzug*] of beings as a whole leaves behind it an 'emptiness as a whole'.[6] *Dasein* is not able to establish a meaningful relationship with beings. It is overwhelmed by total indifference. Nothing holds its attention. All 'possibilities of doing and acting' escape it.[7] This is what constitutes the 'need as a whole'.[8] Where beings withdraw themselves as a whole, time becomes empty. Boredom radically changes the perception of time:

> All beings withdraw from us without exception in every respect [*Hinsicht*], everything we look at . . . everything in retrospect [*Rücksicht*], all beings that we look back upon as having been and having become and as past . . . all beings in every prospect [*Absicht*], everything we look at prospectively as futural . . .'[9]

If we translate the three perspectives on beings into temporal terms, they are the past (retrospection [*Rücksicht*]), the present (inspection [*Hinsicht*]) and future (prospection [*Absicht*]). In the condition of profound boredom, *Dasein* cannot establish any temporal relationship with beings. But meaning consists in relationships. Thus, profound boredom is experienced as the total absence of meaning. It derives from the emptiness of time. Where no temporal perspective on beings is possible, time becomes amorphous, or a simple mass. There is no possibility of the kind of temporal articulation that would allow time to appear as meaningful.

The telling refusal [*Versagen*] of beings as a whole is at the same time, according to Heidegger, a '*telling*' [*Sagen*]. The falling away of all 'possibilities of doing and acting'[10] in the condition of profound boredom leads to the 'dawning' of those possibilities to act which *Dasein* could have, but 'which are left unexploited precisely in this "it is boring for one"'.[11] The 'telling announcement' [*Ansagen*] in the telling refusal takes place as a '*calling*' which calls upon *Dasein* explicitly to grasp *itself*:

> The self-liberation of Dasein, however, only happens in each case if Dasein *resolutely discloses* [*sich entschließt*] itself *to itself* . . . To the extent, however, that Dasein finds itself disposed in the midst of beings, . . . Dasein can resolutely disclose itself only . . . if it resolutely discloses itself for action here and now . . . in this chosen and essential possibility of its self. This *resolute self-disclosure* of Dasein to itself . . . is the *moment of vision* [*Augenblick*].[12]

The redeeming moment of vision is the '*look of resolute disclosedness* [*Blick der Entschlossenheit*]', the look of *Dasein* when it 'discloses itself for action here and now'.[13] Heidegger is confident that this heroic resolution to act, in which *Dasein* properly grasps itself, has the power to break the entrancement of profound boredom. In his lecture course of 1929/30, Heidegger assumed that only the resolution to act is able to remove the emptiness of being, even the emptiness of time. He did not yet realize that it is *precisely* the emphasis on acting, the resolution to take action, even the freedom of the *initium* itself, that are responsible for the emptiness of time, namely for the fact that time no longer founds a fulfilled duration.

Although Heidegger, in his lectures of 1929/30, pointed out that, especially in Alemannic usage, "'to have long time" means the same as "to be homesick"',[14] and that profound boredom therefore is the longing for home [*Zug zur Heimat*], he did not pursue this suspected proximity of boredom to homesickness any further in these lectures. And he did not yet recognize that the subjectivity of a *Dasein* that is determined to act cannot found a home, that it actually means the end of home.

Thirty years later, the closeness between profound boredom and homesickness once again comes to Heidegger's attention:

It [i.e. home; *'die Heimat'*] still is and concerns us, but *as the one we are looking for*. For presumably it is the little noticed fundamental mood of profound boredom which drives us into all these distractions [*Zeitvertreib*] offered every day by the strange, stimulating, bewitching things belonging to what is not of the home [*Unheimische*]. What is more: Presumably, this profound boredom – in the form of the addiction to distractions – is the hidden, unacknowledged, pushed aside and yet inescapable longing for home: hidden homesickness.[15]

Time loses duration, that which lasts long and what is slow. Because it does not hold the attention for long, empty intervals emerge, which must be bridged with the help of drastic and stimulating means. Thus, boredom is accompanied by the 'mania for what is surprising, for what immediately sweeps [us] away and impresses [us], again and again in different ways'.[16]

Fulfilled presence gives way to 'the restlessness of the always inventive operation [*Getriebe*]'.[17] Heidegger no longer juxtaposes the determination to act with profound boredom. He now understands that the 'look of resolute disclosedness' is *too short-sighted* and cannot capture that which lasts long and what is slow, the fragrant length of time; he understands that it is precisely an exaggerated subjectivity which makes profound boredom possible in the first place – that not more of the self, but more of the world, not more of activity, but more of lingering can break the spell of boredom.

Boredom dominates the widening gap between subject and world, between freedom and facticity, between action and being. The *Dasein* that is determined to act is no longer familiar with the feeling of being-surrounded [*Umfangenwerden*] or of being-taken-in [*Eingeholtwerden*]. The 'point' of the 'moment' [*Augenblick*], as the temporal form of the self, lacks the width and length of 'home', the space for dwelling and lingering. Heidegger's 'home' signifies the place which precedes the acting subject, the place to which one *entrusts* [*anheimgeben*] oneself and which has always already taken in the acting self. The determination to act precisely lets *Dasein* slide away from the place that precedes subjectivity. Profound boredom derives from the loss of this place.

In the later Heidegger, the emphasis on acting is taken back in favour of an entirely different relationship with the world that is called 'releasement' [*Gelassenheit*]. Releasement is a counter-movement, even a 'counter-rest', to the determination to act.[18] Releasement grants us 'the possibility of dwelling [*aufhalten*] in the world in a totally different way'.[19] Concepts such as 'hesitancy',[20] 'timidity' [*Scheu*] or 'restraint'[21] are also turns against the emphasis on acting. In the end, the responsibility for profound boredom lies with a life that is fully dominated by the determination to act. Profound boredom is the flip side of excessive activity, of a *vita activa* that lacks any form of contemplation. A compulsive activism keeps boredom alive. The spell of profound boredom will only be genuinely broken if the *vita activa* incorporates the *vita contemplativa* into its critical pole and once again serves the latter.

12

Vita Contemplativa

I. A BRIEF HISTORY OF LEISURE [*MUSSE*]

We have a bed, we have a child,
my lady!
We also have work, yours and mine,
have the sun, rain, and the wind so mild.
One small thing only is missing, oh lady fine,
for being as free as the birds: And that is time.

Richard Dehmel, *The Worker*

Heidegger is said to have opened one of his lectures on Aristotle by saying: 'Aristotle was born, worked, and died.'[1] It is surprising that Heidegger would characterize Aristotle's life as work. He must have known that the life of a philosopher – as a *bios theoretikos* – was anything but work. According to Aristotle, philosophizing – as *theorein* – owes its existence to leisure (*schole*). The meaning of the Greek *schole* has little to do with today's 'idleness' or 'leisure time'. It is a state of freedom, without coercion or necessitation, without toil or care. Work, by contrast, takes away freedom, because it is subject to the coercive force exerted by the necessities of life. As opposed to leisure, it does not rest in itself, because it must produce what is useful and necessary.

Aristotle divided life into two areas, into time employed for non-leisure (*a-scholia*) and time of leisure (*schole*), that is, into non-rest and rest. Work as non-rest, as un-freedom, must be subordinated to leisure. With regard to activities (*prakta*), Aristotle also situated the beautiful and noble outside of what is useful and necessary, that is, outside of work.[2] Only need forces work upon us; work is therefore *need*-ful. Leisure, by contrast, opens up a space beyond the necessities of life that is free of compulsion and care. According to Aristotle, the nature of human existence is not care, but leisure. Contemplative rest enjoys absolute priority. All activities have to be carried out with the aim of this rest in mind and have to return to it.

Aristotle distinguishes three forms of life (*bioi*) of the *free* man: the life of striving for pleasure (*hedone*), that of producing beautiful and noble deeds in the polis (*bios politikos*), and that which is dedicated to the contemplation of truth (*bios theoretikos*).[3] All three of them are free from the needs and compulsions of life. The life dedicated to making money is set aside on account of its compulsive character. The *bios politikos* is not dedicated to the organization of communal life, because this would involve man in necessary and useful things. Rather, it strives for honour and virtue. Skills such as drawing and painting are to be acquired because they promote the ability to contemplate physical beauty.[4] The highest form of happiness has its source in the contemplative lingering on beauty, the activity that used to be called *theoria*. Its temporal dimension is duration. It turns towards those things that are imperishable and unchanging, the things that rest entirely in themselves. Only the contemplative devotion to truth, not virtue and not prudence, brings man close to the gods.

Work is bound up with the necessities of life. It is not an end in itself but a means, even a necessary one, a means of life that turns needs away [*not-wendendes Lebens-Mittel*]. It is therefore not worthy of a free man. Were someone of noble descent forced by needs to work, he would have to hide the fact. Work makes him unfree. Leisure is a condition in which there is no care, no need, no compulsion. A human being only becomes properly human in this condition. The ancient notion of leisure is based on a project of *Dasein* which is inaccessible, even unintelligible, to us today; we live in a world that is altogether absorbed by work, efficiency and productivity. The ancient culture of leisure opens up the prospect for us of the possibility of an entirely different world, a world in which the fundamental trait of human *Dasein* would not be care, as it is for Heidegger. The concept of work on which Heidegger's remark on Aristotle's life is based emerged only late in history. It belongs to the realm of the Protestant view of life and would have been wholly alien to Aristotle. What Heidegger actually should have said is: 'Aristotle was born, did *not* work, and died.'

Leisure, being *schola*, is outside of work *and* outside of inactivity. It is a special ability and requires a specific education. It is not a practice of 'relaxation' or of 'switching off'. Thinking, as *theorein*, as the contemplative consideration of truth, is based on leisure.[5] Thus, St Augustine distinguishes leisure (*otium*) from passive inertia: 'The attraction of a life of leisure ought not to be the prospect of a lazy inactivity, but the chance for the investigation and discovery of truth.' The 'praiseworthy kind of leisure' entails 'the pursuit of truth'.[6] The incapacity for leisure is precisely a sign of inertia. Leisure is not the neighbour of lazy inactivity; it is its opposite. It does not serve the purpose of distraction, but of collecting oneself. Lingering presupposes a gathering of the senses.

In the Middle Ages, *vita contemplativa* still maintained priority over *vita activa*. Thus, Aquinas wrote: 'Vita contemplativa simpliciter melior est quam activa' [the contemplative life is simply more excellent than the active].[7] The well-known dictum *ora et labora* does not express an appreciation of work over contemplation. In the Middle Ages, the *vita activa* was still altogether imbued with the *vita contemplativa*. Work was given its meaning by contemplation. The day began with prayers. And prayers ended it. They provided a temporal rhythm. An altogether different significance attached to the festive days. They were not days off work. As times of prayer and of leisure they had their own significance. The medieval calendar did not just serve the purpose of *counting* days. Rather, it was based on a *story* in which the festive days represent narrative resting points. They are fixed points within the flow of time, providing narrative bonds so that the time does not simply elapse. The festive days form temporal sections which structure time and give it a rhythm. They function like the sections of a story, and let time and its passing appear meaningful. Each section of a story completes a narrative section, and this provisional completion prepares the next stage of the narrative. The temporal sections are meaningful transitions within an overall narrative frame. The time of hope, the time of joy, and the time of farewell merge into each other.

The attitude towards work begins to change in the late Middle Ages. Thomas More's *Utopia*, for instance, paints a picture of a world in which everyone works. His revolutionary project for a new society is aimed against class distinctions and suggests a just distribution of work. Everyone needs to work for only six hours every day. In their time away from work, the 'utopians' dedicate themselves to leisure and contemplation. But the value of work as such is not actually increased by this design. Only in the context of the Reformation does work acquire an importance which far exceeds that of fulfilling the necessities of life. It is now put in the context of a theological meaning that serves to legitimate it and raise its value. In Luther, work as a vocation is associated with God's calling upon men. In Calvinism, work is given meaning in the context of the economy of salvation. A Calvinist is uncertain whether or not he or she is chosen or condemned. Thus, anxiety and permanent care [*Sorge*] dominate the acting of the individual, who is left entirely to his own devices. Only success in work is interpreted as a sign of having been chosen. The care for salvation turns the individual into a worker. Although this restless labour cannot achieve salvation, it is the only means of assuring oneself of having been chosen, and thus of reducing anxiety.

Calvinism develops an emphasis on acting and on determined activity: 'The religious believer can make himself sure of his state of grace *either* in that he feels himself to be the vessel of the Holy Spirit or the tool of the divine will. In the former case his religious life tends to mysticism and emotionalism, in the latter to ascetic action.'[8] A Calvinist attains the certainty of his salvation by acting with resolve. The seeker of salvation is brought closer to his goal not by a *vita contemplativa*, but by a *vita activa*. With the raising of the determination to act to the level of an absolute value, the *vita contemplativa* appears reprehensible.

The inner-worldly asceticism of Protestantism connects work with salvation. Work increases the glory of God. It becomes the purpose of life. Max Weber quotes the Pietist Zinzendorf: 'One does not only work in order to live, but one lives for the sake of one's work, and if there is no more work to do one suffers or goes to sleep.'[9] Wasting time is the worst of all sins. Extending the hours of sleep unnecessarily is also condemned. The economy of time and that of salvation become intermingled. The Calvinist Baxter writes:

Keep up a high esteem of time and be every day more careful that you lose none of your time, than you are that you lose none of your gold and silver. And if vain recreation, dressings, feastings, idle talk, unprofitable company, or sleep, be any of them temptations to rob you of any of your time, accordingly heighten your watchfulness.[10]

Max Weber sees the spirit of capitalism prefigured in Protestant asceticism. The latter finds expression in a compulsion to accumulate which leads to the formation of capital. It is considered reprehensible to rest on one's laurels and just enjoy one's wealth. Only the continual striving for more profit is agreeable to God:

This worldly Protestant asceticism ... acted powerfully against the spontaneous enjoyment of possessions; it restricted *consumption*, especially of luxuries. On the other hand, it had the psychological effect of freeing the acquisition of goods from the inhibitions of traditionalistic ethics. It broke the bonds of the impulse of acquisition in that it not only legalized it, but ... looked upon it as directly willed by God.[11]

The process of secularization did not lead to the disappearance of the economy of salvation. The latter is still alive in modern capitalism. Material greed alone does not explain the focus on the acquisition of money, which appears almost irrational. The compulsion towards accumulation is based on a striving towards salvation. By making investments, the actual speculation aims at salvation. The latter's content can take diverse forms. Apart from the desire to have infinitely more time at one's disposal than one's own limited lifetime through the endless amassing of money as congealed time, the urge towards wealth accumulation is also produced by the striving for power. The very word 'wealth' [*Vermögen*] is telling.[12] An increase in wealth in the form of capital also increases the range of what one is able to do. For Marx, money is all-powerful in that it brings about a de-facticization; it suspends thrownness [*Geworfenheit*] in favour of projectedness [*Entworfenheit*]. Money effects a general suspension of what is factually given. It even suspends ugliness:

> That which exists for me through the medium of *money*, that which I can pay for, i.e. which money can buy, that *am* I, the possessor of the money. The stronger the power of my money, the stronger am I. The properties of money are my, the possessor's, properties and essential powers. Therefore what I *am* and what I *can do* is by no means determined by my individuality. I *am* ugly, but I can buy the *most beautiful* woman. Which means to say that I am not *ugly*, for the effect of *ugliness*, its repelling power, is destroyed by money.[13]

The word 'industry' derives from the Latin term *industria*, which means 'diligence'. The English word 'industry' retains the meaning of 'diligence' and 'busy activity' to the present day. 'Industrial School', for instance, meant 'reformatory'. Industrialization not only meant the mechanization of the world, but also the disciplining of human beings. It installed not only machines, but also dispositifs that optimized human behaviour, even optimized the physical body itself, in the interest of temporal and labour efficiency. Typically enough, a treatise of 1768 by Philipp Peter Guden is called 'Polizey der Industrie, oder Abhandlung von den Mitteln, den Fleiß der Einwohner zu ermuntern' [The policing of industry, or: treatise on the means for encouraging the diligence of inhabitants].

With the process of industrialization as mechanization, human temporality approaches the temporality of machines.

The industrial dispositif is an imperative of temporal efficiency that has the task of forming the human being according to the timing of the machine. It aligns human life to the mechanical working process – to functioning. Life dominated by work is a *vita activa* which is entirely cut off from the *vita contemplativa*. If the human being loses all capacity for contemplation, it degenerates into an *animal laborans*. The life which adjusts itself to the mechanical work process knows only breaks, work-free interim periods in which the regeneration from work takes place in order to be fully available again for the process of work. Thus, 'relaxation' and 'switching off' do not constitute a counterbalance to work. They are integrated into the work process, in the sense that they primarily serve the purpose of re-establishing the ability to work.

The so-called society of leisure and consumption does not bring about an essential change in work. It is not free from the imperative to work. The source of the compulsion is, in this case, no longer the necessities of life but work itself. Hannah Arendt erroneously assumes that the telos of the society of labourers is the freedom of the human being from the 'fetters' of labour.[14] In reality, this society is one in which labour, independent of the necessities of life, becomes an end in itself and posits itself as absolute. Work is totalized to such a degree that outside of working hours the only time that remains is that which is to be 'killed'. The totalization of labour pushes out all other forms of life and life projects. It forces the mind itself to work. 'Intellectual labour' is a formula of compulsion. The *mind* that works would be a contradiction.

The society of consumption and leisure is characterized by a particular temporality. Surplus time, which is the result of a massive increase in productivity, is filled with events and experiences that are fleeting and short-lived. As nothing binds time in a lasting fashion, the impression is created that

92

time is passing very quickly, or that everything is accelerating. Consumption and duration contradict each other. Consumer goods do not last. They are marked by decay as their constitutive element, and the cycles of appearance and decay become ever shorter. The capitalist imperative of growth means that things are produced and consumed with increasing speed. The compulsion to consume is immanent to the system of production. Economic growth depends on the quick uptake and consumption of things. As the economy is organized with growth in mind, it would completely grind to a halt if people suddenly began to take care of things, to protect them against decay and to make sure that they endure.

In the consumer society, one forgets how to linger. Consumer goods do not permit a contemplative lingering. They are used up as quickly as possible in order to create space for new products and needs. Contemplative lingering presupposes things which endure. But the compulsion to consume does away with duration. Neither, however, does so-called deceleration found duration. As far as the attitude to consumption is concerned, 'slow food' does not essentially differ from 'fast food'. Things are consumed – no more, no less. A reduction in speed does not by itself transform the *being* of things. The real problem is that all that endures, all that lasts and is slow, threatens to disappear altogether, or to be absent from life. Forms of the *vita contemplativa* are also modes of being, such as 'hesitancy', 'releasement', 'shyness', 'waiting' or 'restraint', which the later Heidegger juxtaposed to the 'stupidity of simply working'.[15] These modes all rest on an experience of duration. But the time of work, even time as work, is without duration. It *consumes* time for production. What lasts and is slow, however, evades being used up and consumed. It founds a duration. The *vita contemplativa* is a practice of duration. It founds an *other time* by interrupting the *time of work*.

II. THE MASTER–SLAVE DIALECTIC

And write with confidence: 'In the beginning was the deed'!
But make sure to put the emphasis in the right place: In the
beginning was the deed; because all higher development is
guided by the will to laziness.

Georg Simmel[16]

The revaluation of work, which in the course of modern
times leads to work's absolute status, even to its glorification,
is a very complex and multilayered phenomenon. This revaluation happened not only for religious reasons, but also for
reasons to do with economic power. Max Weber's sociology
of religion neglects this dimension of the logic of power. The
causal interrelations between labour, capital, power, domination and salvation are deeply entangled. The economy of
salvation and the economy of power permeate each other.

From the point of view of the economy of power, the
totalization of work can be described as a consequence of the
dialectic between master and slave, which, however, needs to
be explained in an entirely different way than is familiar from
Hegel's story. As is well known, what Hegel describes under
that rubric is a life-and-death struggle at the end of which one
party *works* as the slave for the other as his master. According
to Hegel's thesis, it is the fear of death which makes the
future slave enter into submission to the other party. The
future slave prefers submission to death, and clings on to
life, while the master desires more than pure life. The master
strives for power and freedom. In contrast to the slave, the
master does not posit pure life, but his self as absolute. This is
an act of self-totalization by way of the total negation of the
other. The other, who is now the slave of the master, does
not diminish the self, the power, of the master, because he
or she has entered into submission to the master. The master

extends his self into the slave, and the slave gives up his self to the self of the master. Thus, the master is fully with himself in the slave, and this continuity of the self constitutes the power of the master.

The dialectic of work as the dialectic of power consists in the fact that the slave, who performs forced labour in order just to survive, nevertheless also gains an idea of freedom precisely through this work. His production of things is a form of labour that imposes his own characteristics on nature by forming it. The things produced have the form of the slave himself. He submits nature to himself. To begin with, nature makes itself felt through its resistance, which the slave breaks through his appropriation of nature. His labour conveys ideas of power and freedom to him; these ideas differ from the pure survival for the sake of which he once submitted to the master. Thus, work 'forms' [*bildet*] him.[17] It is the medium in which the formation of consciousness takes place, and it liberates the slave. Labour conveys an *idea* of freedom to him, which he will have to *realize* in the course of history through class struggles. And he will not evade these struggles.

Hegel's dialectic of master and slave considers everything exclusively from the perspective of power and subjectivity. This is its crucial weakness. From this perspective, nothing but power determines the relationships with things. Through his labour the slave takes possession of the independent existence of things. He *works* away their resistance. The things which he *works* on [*be*-arbeitet] are consumed by the master. For both the master and the slave the relationship to things is that of *negation*. Not only work, but also consumption negates independent being. But one important aspect of work is entirely ignored in Hegel's dialectic of master and slave. The slave, by taking wholly upon himself the arduous work that reveals to him the resistance of the things, makes possible for the master a different relationship to things – a relationship

95

that is neither one of domination, nor work [*Bearbeiten*]. The master thus realizes that power or negation are not the only possible relationships to things.

Labour occupies a central place in Hegel. Not 'divine cognition' or 'disporting', but the 'labour of the negative' is the mode which characterizes the process of spirit.[18] Kojève, in his Marxist interpretation of Hegel's master–slave dialectic, also declares labour to be the chief medium of education and history: 'This creative education of Man by work (*Bildung*) creates History – i.e., human Time. Work is Time.'[19] There is no time that is not work. Work *is* time. Work gives consciousness its form, and it drives history forwards: 'Consequently, History stops at the moment when the difference, the opposition, between Master and Slave disappears.'[20] Work is the agent of history. Thus, the working slave advances to the position of the sole subject of historical progress. It follows that the master, by contrast, freezes into an inactive and unproductive identity. Because the slave is the sole acting subject of history, it is the slave alone who determines the course of history. In this, the slave remains a labourer throughout all of his developmental stages. At no point in history does labour exceed itself. It remains the same at all times and without exception, acting as a *dispositif* which can take moral, economic or religious forms. The working slave uses this dispositif specifically in order to turn the power relation upside down, and thus to his favour. Its increasing importance eventually makes it a predominant social dispositif. The society with which history reaches its completion is accordingly a society of labour – a society in which everyone works, even does nothing but work. As a result of the totalization of labour *everyone* will become a labourer at the end of history.

Aristotle distinguished between three kinds of life. A *free* man may choose between them. The highest form of life is the *bios theoretikos*, a life dedicated to contemplation. As a free man, the master does not come into direct contact with the resistance exerted by things, as he leaves all work to the slave. This freedom enables him to have an entirely different relationship to the world, one that is not determined by the world as an object of work or domination. The contemplative relationship to things presupposes freedom from work. It interrupts the time that is *work*. According to Aristotle, the *vita contemplativa* is divine because it does not suffer any compulsion and is free from any interest.

With regard to the totalization of work, Marx represents the completion of Hegel. According to Marx, it is not thinking but work that distinguishes man from the animal. The human being is not *animal rationale*, but *animal laborans*. The human being *is* work. Marx also interprets Hegel's *Phenomenology of Spirit* from the perspective of work:

> The importance of Hegel's Phenomenology and its final result – the dialectic of negativity as the moving and producing principle – lies in the fact that Hegel . . . grasps the nature of *labour* and conceives objective man – true, because real man – as the result of his *own labour* . . . Hegel adopts the standpoint of modern political economy.[21]

Marx could have simply said: *spirit is labour*. Hegel's spirit, *like his slave*, is under a compulsion to work. It has no time for leisure or contemplation. The dispositif of work captures thinking itself and appears as a dispositif of thinking. Because its original aim is the domination of things, thinking that *works* remains the authoritarian thinking of domination [*Herrschaftsdenken*].

The slave is liberated from the domination of the master, but at the price of becoming a slave to work. Everyone is caught by the dispositif of work – masters and slaves alike. Thus, a society of work emerges in which *everyone* is a slave to work, i.e. a society of working people. Everything has to be a kind of work, and there is no time that is not dedicated to work. The dispositif of work makes *time itself do work*. Work makes use of all activities and forces for itself; it presents itself as *one universal* activity. Because all energy is fully absorbed by work, the only thing that can fill the time outside of work is a passive entertainment or recreation that serves only to make the worker able to work again with his full strength.

The society of work is ultimately a society of compulsion. Work does *not* set you free. The dispositif of work creates a new form of servitude. As long as consciousness remains dominated by the dispositif of work, Hegel's dialectic of master and slave, as a dialectic of freedom, will nevertheless not bring about a free society. For this reason, we may say that the dialectical history of the formation of consciousness was not thought through to its end by Hegel. Consciousness will only be fully free if it also liberates itself from the imperative of work. This imperative makes the forms of life of the free man, i.e. the forms of leisure (*schole*), disappear altogether. What is posited as absolute is activity as non-rest (*a-scholia*), whereas, according to Aristotle, the latter needs to be wholly subordinated to rest (*schole*). Today, the relationship between rest (*schole*) and non-rest (*ascholia*) has been reversed. Rest now is a time of recreation or relaxation that is necessary for the sake of work.

History – which, according to Hegel, is a history of freedom – will not be completed as long as we remain the slaves of work. The domination of work makes us unfree. The opposition between master and slave cannot be sublated by *everyone* becoming a slave of work. It will only be removed if the slave actually transforms himself into a *free* man. The *vita activa* remains a term of compulsion as long as it does not incorporate the *vita contemplativa* within itself. A *vita activa* that lacks any contemplative moment becomes empty and turns into pure activity, leading to franticness and restlessness. Georg Simmel holds that history will not reach its end with a society of 'full employment', but with a society that finds the *leisure* necessary for reaching an endpoint:

> That play of cosmic forces which is guided by the law of an energy that preserves itself, moves toward a final point: one day, our scientists tell us, all differences in temperature within the cosmos will be balanced out; all atoms will be in a state of equilibrium, and all energy will be distributed evenly across everything that exists. At that point, the saeculum of movement will have reached its end and the eternal kingdom of cosmic laziness will begin. Thus, the latter is the final goal of the order of earthly things, set by that order itself. And it constitutes man's greatness and dignity that he can anticipate and realize this goal in himself by becoming – in his laziest hours – a microcosm in the most essential sense, because the final goal of cosmic development then has become spirit, feeling, enjoyment in him. By becoming conscious of this, philosophy has reached the *farthest point in its history*, after which all it can do is remain silent, in order, thus – having finally done justice to its task – for the first time to represent in itself the principle which it has recognized as the absolute principle in the world.[22]

Despite the central importance of labour for Marx, his utopia is not based on a glorification of it. Occasionally, he even has in mind the liberation from labour: 'Free time – which is both idle time and time for higher activity – has naturally transformed its possessor into a different subject, and he then enters into the direct production process as this different subject.'[23] It is Hegel's central insight that labour not only transforms the world, but also the labouring subject. Thus, labour helps the slave gain a more developed consciousness,

99

which elevates him above animal life. However, given the preponderance of labour, which Marx declares to be the characteristic trait of the human being,[24] it is highly questionable whether that being is really capable of transforming itself into a 'different subject', a subject which would be able to engage in that *free* time which is no longer a *time of labour*.

Due to its descent, the subject of Marx remains a subject of labour. Even when it does not work, it is not capable of an altogether different kind of activity. Outside of work, it is at best a consumer. Labourer and consumer are related to each other. Both *use up* time. They have no access to the *vita contemplativa*. Hannah Arendt considers it a blatant contradiction that Marx 'in all stages of his work . . . defines man as an *animal laborans* and then leads him into a society in which this greatest and most human power is no longer necessary'.[25] One might respond to Arendt by saying that Marx distinguishes between alienated or forced labour and free labour, and by holding that the liberation from work applies only to the former. But labour as such only allows for a very narrow relationship towards oneself and the world. A subject that is formed through or by work will not find a different perception of the world during times that are free from work.

The production and consumption of things as the only possible activities of the labouring subject is opposed to the contemplative lingering on things. Today's society, in particular, is proof of the fact that a human being that has become nothing but a subject of labour is incapable of engaging with that *free* time which is not a time of labour. Although increasing productivity creates more and more free time, this time is used neither for higher activities nor for leisure. Rather, it serves the purpose either of recreation outside of work or of consumption. The *animal laborans* is familiar only with breaks, but not with contemplative rest. The dialectic between master and slave is only complete as a dialectic of freedom if it transcends the realm of labour – if it retains the remembrance of the *other of labour*.

III. *VITA ACTIVA* OR ON ACTIVE LIFE

... andante ... the tempo of a passionate and slow spirit – ...
Friedrich Nietzsche[26]

Hannah Arendt's *The Human Condition* is dedicated to a rehabilitation, even revitalization, of the notion of an 'active life', which, according to her, is increasingly withering away. She makes the problematic assumption that the primacy of contemplation in the Greek and Christian tradition is responsible for the 'very restricted dignity' bestowed upon '*vita activa*'. The primacy of *vita contemplativa*, she argues, reduces all forms of *vita activa* to the level of useful and necessary labour:

> My contention is simply that the enormous weight of contemplation in the traditional hierarchy has blurred the distinctions and articulations within the *vita activa* itself and that, appearances notwithstanding, this condition has not been changed essentially by the modern break with the tradition and the eventual reversal of its hierarchical order in Marx and Nietzsche.[27]

Against this levelling of the *vita activa*, Arendt feels that she needs to illuminate the various forms in which it appears, with the emphasis in her phenomenology of the *vita activa* being on the life which is determined to act.

It is erroneous to assume that the primacy of contemplation is responsible for the reduction of the *vita activa* to labour. Rather, we must assume that human action is reduced to mere activity and labour precisely by losing all of its contemplative aspects. Arendt mistakenly represents contemplation

101

as an arresting of all movement and action, as a passive rest which makes any form of *vita activa* appear as restlessness. Mortals, she writes, achieve contemplation, 'when all human movements and activities are at perfect rest'.[28] This immobility concerns the body as well as the soul: 'Every movement, the movement of body and soul as well as of speech and reasoning, must cease before truth.'[29] Arendt does not see that the *vita contemplativa* represents a form of rest only because it rests *in itself*. But rest-in-itself does not therefore have to be without movement or action. God also rests in himself. But he is pure act (*actus purus*). The *in-itself* here only means that there is no dependence on anything outside; it means that one is *free*. Thus, Aristotle explicitly calls the contemplative life (*bios theoretikos*) an *active* life, because thinking as *theoria* is an *energeia*, literally meaning work-activity or being-at-work (*en ergô einai*). Thomas Aquinas follows Aristotle in this: 'External bodily movements are opposed to the quiet of *contemplation*, which consists in rest from outward occupations: but the movements of *intellectual* operations belong to the quiet of *contemplation*.'[30]

Arendt's rehabilitation of the *vita activa* is primarily concerned with acting which she charges with heroic pathos. To act means to begin something altogether new. Without the determination to act, the human being atrophies into a *homo laborans*. Being-born is not being-thrown, but being-capable-of-acting. Arendt's heroism of acting even reaches a Messianic crescendo:

> The miracle that saves the world . . . is ultimately the fact of natality, in which the faculty of action is ontologically rooted. It is, in other words, the birth of new men and the new beginning, the action they are capable of by virtue of being born . . . It is this faith in and hope for the world that found perhaps its most glorious and most succinct expres-

sion in the few words with which the Gospels announced their 'glad tidings': 'A child has been born unto us.'[31]

In temporal terms, acting means letting time begin anew. Its essence is revolution. A revolution 'interrupts' 'the inexorable automatic course of daily life'.[32] In the face of the natural time of repetition, a new beginning is a 'miracle'. Acting is a genuinely human 'miracle-working faculty'.[33] But Arendt erroneously believes that what is really new owes its coming about exclusively to a heroic subject that is determined to act. But these events which form the world and culture rarely derive from the conscious decision taken by a subject choosing to act. Rather, they are often the product of leisure, of play free from compulsion or of the free imagination.[34]

Arendt's emphatic idea of acting is conceived in light of the historical process that sees the human being degenerate into an *animal laborans*. Her thesis is that in modernity human life takes the form of a collective life process which does not offer any space for individual action. All that is expected of human beings is an automatic functioning,

> as though individual life had actually been submerged in the over-all life process of the species and the only active decision still required of the individual were to let go, so to speak, to abandon his individuality ... and acquiesce in a dazed, 'tranquilized', functional type of behaviour.[35]

Labour inserts the individual into the life process of the species, a process which continues beyond individual acts and decisions.

Against the passivity of the *animal laborans*, Arendt invokes acting. Active life is juxtaposed with the 'deadliest, most sterile passivity' in which modern times, after beginning with such promise by enlivening all human faculties, threatens to

103

end.[36] But Arendt fails to recognize that the passivity of the *animal laborans* is not the opposite of active life, but precisely its reverse side. Seen from that angle, the emphasis on active life which Arendt associates with acting does not form a counter-force to the passivity of the *animal laborans*, because being active agrees very well with the collective life process of the species. In one of his aphorisms, titled *Main deficiency of active people*, Nietzsche writes:

> Active men are usually lacking in higher activity – I mean individual activity. They are active as officials, businessmen, scholars, that is, as generic beings, but not as quite particular, single and unique men. In this respect they are lazy . . . Active people roll like a stone, conforming to the stupidity of mechanics.[37]

Arendt notes that modern life increasingly turns away from the *vita contemplativa*, but she does not give this any further thought. She makes the *vita contemplativa* responsible for the indiscriminate levelling of all forms of the *vita activa* as mere labour, but does not recognize that the franticness and restlessness of modern life has a lot to do with the loss of the contemplative faculty. The totalization of the *vita activa* also contributes to the 'loss of human experience' which Arendt herself deplores.[38] Just being active impoverishes your experience. It continues ever the same. Whoever is not capable of stopping and pausing has no access to what is altogether different. Experience transforms. It interrupts the repetition of the ever same. You do not become more susceptible to the making of experiences by becoming more active. Rather, what is needed is a particular kind of passivity. You need to let yourself be *concerned* with that which evades the activity of the acting subject: 'To undergo an experience with something – be it a thing, a person, or a god – means that this something befalls us, strikes us, comes over us, overwhelms and transforms us.'[39]

Arendt's attitude towards time is thoroughly characterized by domination over it. Forgiveness, as an emphatic act, is a 'power' which consists in the ability to let time begin anew, and thus it frees the acting subject from the past, from a temporal burden which tries to pin it down forever.[40] Promising makes the future calculable and available by protecting it against unpredictability. With the force of forgiveness and promising, the acting subject seizes time. Its character as a power connects acting deeply with other forms of the *vita activa*, namely with producing and labouring. The important faculty of 'interfering' is not only a feature that belongs to acting, but also to producing and labouring.[41]

Being cannot be reduced to being active. Even acting itself must contain moments of pausing in order not to freeze into mere labour. In the breathturn [*Atemwende*][42] of acting lies a stillness. Upon pausing before an action, at the moment of hesitation, the acting subject becomes aware of the immeasurable space that lies in front of the decision to act. The contingency of an action impresses itself fully on the acting subject only at the moment of its hesitating retreat from the action. A determination to act that does not know how to hesitate is blind. It sees neither its own shadow nor the other of itself. Although hesitation is not a positive act in itself, it is constitutive of the act. What distinguishes acting from labouring is not a surplus of activity, but the capacity to pause. Whoever does not know how to hesitate is a labourer.

Towards the end of *The Human Condition*, Arendt unexpectedly invokes thought. Thought, she says, was probably least damaged by that development in modern times which is responsible for the 'victory of the *animal laborans*'. Although the future of the world will not depend on thought, but on the 'power of acting individuals', thought will nevertheless not be irrelevant for the human future: when looking at the 'various activities within the *vita activa*' with regard to 'the extent of sheer activity' involved, 'it might well be that thinking as such would surpass them all'.[43] However, Arendt leaves it altogether unclear why the experience of being active should find its purest expression in thinking. In what sense is thinking more active than the most active deed? Isn't thinking the most active of all activities precisely because it reaches great heights and falls to great depths, because of all activities it ventures the furthest, and because – as con-*templation* – it gathers the vastest spaces and temporal distances in itself, in a word: because it is contemplative?

Thinking, in the sense of *theoria*, is a contemplative activity. It is a manifestation of the *vita contemplativa*. Paradoxically, Arendt elevates it to the level of an activity which exceeds other activities of the *vita activa* in terms of sheer being active. For Aristotle, the activity of thinking is divine because it frees itself from any action, that is, because it is contemplative:

> We assume the gods to be supremely blessed and happy; but what sorts of action should we attribute to them? Just actions? . . . Courageous acts, then, enduring what is fearful and facing dangers because it is noble to do so? . . . So if we remove from a living being the possibility of action . . . what is left apart from contemplation? So the god's activity, which is superior in blessedness, will be contemplative. . .[44]

Arendt ends her book with a remark by Cato to which Cicero refers in his *De Re Publica*: 'Never is he more active than when he does nothing, never is he less alone than when he is by himself.'[45] This remark actually refers to the *vita contemplativa*. Arendt turns it into praise for the *vita activa*. She apparently misses the point that this 'solitude' is also dedicated to the *vita contemplativa*, that it is diametrically opposed to collective action and the 'power of acting individuals'. In the passage following the quotation, Cicero explicitly asks his readers to retreat from the 'crowded forum' into the solitude of a contemplative life. Thus, immediately after quoting Cato, he praises the *vita contemplativa*. Not an active, but a contemplative life, committed to the eternal and divine, is what first turns the human being into what it is meant to be:

> What power, what office, what kingdom can be grander than to look down on all things human and to think of them as less important than wisdom, and to turn over in his mind nothing except what is eternal and divine? Such a man believes that others may be called human, but that the only true humans are those who have been educated in truly human arts.[46]

Towards the end of her book on the *vita activa*, Arendt involuntarily advocates the *vita contemplativa*. Right until the end, it remains hidden from her that it is precisely the loss of the contemplative faculty which is responsible for the degeneration of the human being into an *animal laborans*.

IV. *VITA CONTEMPLATIVA*, OR OF REFLECTIVE LIFE

All of you, to whom unrestrained labour, and the swift, the new, the strange, are dear, you endure yourselves ill, your industry is flight and will to forget yourselves.
If you believed more in life, you would devote yourselves less to the moment. But you have insufficient capacity for waiting – and even for laziness?

Friedrich Nietzsche[47]

Thinking, Arendt remarks in *The Human Condition*, has always been the privilege of the few. But just for that very reason, they have not become even fewer today.[48] However, this assumption is not entirely correct. It may be a particular characteristic of the present that thinkers, anyhow a small number at any time, have become even fewer. Thinking might have suffered from the fact that the *vita contemplativa* has been pushed aside in favour of the *vita activa*; it is possible that the hyperactive restlessness, the franticness and unrest of today, does not do any good to thinking, and that thinking just reproduces always the same because of increasing time pressures. Nietzsche already lamented the poverty of his times regarding great thinkers, and he explained this poverty with the 'decline and occasional underestimation of the vita contemplativa', with the fact 'that work and industry (formerly attending the great goddess of Health) sometimes seem to rage like a disease'. Because there is 'no time for thinking, and no rest in thinking',[49] divergent views are avoided. They are just hated. The general restlessness does not allow thinking to go deep, to venture far, really to reach for something genuinely different. It is not thinking that dictates to time, but time that dictates to thinking, making it temporary and ephemeral. Thinking no longer communicates with that which lasts. However, Nietzsche believed that 'when the genius of meditation makes a powerful return', this will let his lament fall silent.[50]

Thinking, in the emphatic sense, cannot be accelerated at will. That is where it differs from calculating or from the pure use of the understanding. It often moves in roundabout ways. This is why Kant called wit and acumen 'a kind of intellectual luxury'.[51] The understanding is only concerned with needs and necessity, but not with luxury, which represents a deviation from necessity, even from all things *straight and direct*. A special temporality and spatiality is intrinsic to think-

108

ing that rises above calculating. It does not progress in linear fashion. Thinking is free because its place and time cannot be calculated. It often progresses discontinuously, while calculating follows a linear path. Thus, calculating can be precisely located and, in principle, accelerated at will. Calculating does not look around either. For it, a detour or a step back do not make sense. They only delay the step in the calculation, which is purely a step of the work process. Today, thinking assimilates itself to labour. However, the *animal laborans* is incapable of thinking. For thinking in the emphatic sense, pensive thinking [*sinnendes Denken*], something is required that is not work. Originally, *Sinnen* (Old High German *sinnan*) meant 'journeying' [*Reisen*]. Its *itinerary* is incalculable or discontinuous. Calculating thought is not *on the way*.

Without rest human beings are incapable of seeing what is at rest. Making the *vita activa* an absolute value drives everything out of life that is not an act or activity. The general time pressures destroy all that has the character of a detour, all that is indirect, and thus makes the world poor in forms. Every form, every figure, is a *detour*. Only naked formlessness is direct. If language is deprived of what is indirect in it, its nature approaches that of a scream or an order. Friendliness and politeness are also based on the circuitous and indirect. The orientation of violence, by contrast, is towards directness. If walking lacks all hesitation, all pausing, then it freezes into a march. Time pressures also make what is ambivalent and undecidable, what hovers – the complex or aporetic – give way to a crude distinctness. Nietzsche remarks that the haste of work also makes 'the ear and eye for the melody of movements' disappear.[52] A melody is a detour. Only what is monotonous is direct. Thinking is also marked by a melody. Thinking that entirely lacks any circuitous character degenerates into calculating.

The *vita activa*, which, since the beginning of modern times, has become more and more intense at the expense of the *vita contemplativa*, contributes substantially to the modern compulsion to accelerate. The degradation of the human being to an *animal laborans* can also be interpreted as an effect of this modern development. The emphasis on labour and on acting are *both* based on the primacy of the *vita activa* in modern times and modernity. But Arendt's sharp separation of labour from acting, by interpreting labour as a passive participation in the life of the species, is unjustified. Her concept of acting lacks the evocative power that would have the capacity to break the spell of labour, which degrades the human being to an *animal laborans*, because her emphatic concept of labour is derived from the same primacy of the *vita activa* from which the absolute value of labour is *also* derived. As has repeatedly been stressed, the determination to act and the determination to work share the same genealogical root. Only a revitalization of the *vita contemplativa* would be capable of liberating human beings from the compulsion to labour. In addition, the *animal laborans* is related to the *animal rationale* because the pure exercise of the faculty of understanding is labour. The human being, however, is more than an animal because it possesses the capacity for contemplation, which enables it to communicate with that which lasts, and which, however, does not constitute a class[*Gattung*].

Interestingly, Heidegger devotes little attention to the *vita contemplativa*. All it signifies for him is the meditative-monastic life in contrast to the *vita activa* as the worldly-active one. He reduces contemplation to its rational element, namely categorizing, i.e. analytic seeing,[53] and then associates it with considering [*Betrachtung*].[54] He interprets contemplation from the side of Trachten [striving], the Latin *tractare* which means *to work with* [*behandeln*], or *to refine* [*bearbeiten*] something. According to Heidegger, to strive for something means 'to work one's way toward something, to pursue it, to entrap it in order to secure it'. It follows that contemplation as observation [*Betrachtung*] 'would be an entrapping and securing refining of the real', a 'refining of the real that does encroach uncannily upon it'.[55] Hence, it is a form of *labour*. Despite his closeness to mysticism, Heidegger does not address the mystical dimension of contemplation at all, according to which – as a *lingering with God in loving attentiveness* – it does not possess the categorizing and securing intentionality Heidegger supposes it has. In the *unio mystica*, all divisions and enclosures are precisely removed altogether.

According to Thomas Aquinas, the *vita contemplativa* represents a form of life which makes the human being more perfect: '*In vita contemplativa quaeritur contemplatio veritatis inquantum est perfectio hominis*' ['in the contemplative life the contemplation of truth is sought as being the perfection of man'].[56] Life is impoverished and becomes mere industry [*Gewerbe*] if it loses all contemplative moments. Contemplative lingering interrupts the time which is *labour*: 'work and activity in time are the same' [*werc und gewerbe in der zit und bloz sin des selben*]. The *vita contemplativa* elevates time itself. As opposed to Arendt's claim, there is no one-sided appreciation of the *vita contemplativa* in the Christian tradition. Rather, as in Meister Eckhart, a mediation between *vita activa* and *vita contemplativa* is the goal in mind. Thus, Gregory writes:

> Be aware: while a good plan for life requires that one moves from the active to the contemplative life, it is often useful if the soul returns from the contemplative to the active life, in such a way that the flame of contemplation which has been lit in the heart passes on all its perfection to activity. Thus, active life must lead us to contemplation, but contemplation must set out from what we inwardly considered and call us back to activity.[57]

A *vita contemplativa* without acting is blind, a *vita activa* without contemplation is empty.

Heidegger's later philosophy is dominated by a contemplative mood. The 'Pathway' is a *via contemplativa*, so to speak, on which you do not go anywhere, but rather linger in contemplation. It is no coincidence that Heidegger mentions Meister Eckhart: 'The expanse of all growing things which while along the pathway bestows world. Only in the unspoken of their language – as Eckhart, the old master of letter and life, says – God first becomes God.'[58] By speaking of the 'old master of letter and life', he points towards the necessary mediation between the *vita activa* and *vita contemplativa*. Heidegger uses 'reflection' [*Besinnung*], or 'reflective thought', as contrapuntal terms to the calculating thought that is *labour*. In 'Science and Reflection', he writes: 'Still, the poverty of reflection is the promise of a wealth whose treasures glow in the resplendence of that uselessness which can never be included in any reckoning.'[59] Reflection begins when *thinking that labours stops in its tracks*. Only at the moment of pausing does it traverse the space that lies in front of 'formation'.[60] Only reflection has access to what is not an image, not an idea, but provides the *place* in which they may appear. In its 'surrender to that which is worthy of questioning',[61] it opens itself up to what is slow and takes long, and what evades any quick capture. Reflection widens its gaze by raising it above the present-at and ready-to-hand with which labour is concerned. Where the *hand* stops in the act of capturing, where it hesitates, it acquires a vastness. Thus, Heidegger speaks of a 'hand resting on another person, in which there is concentrated a contact that remains infinitely remote to any touch'.[62] Only in hesitation does an immeasurable space open up for the hand. The hesitating hand is 'suffused and borne by a call calling from afar and calling still farther onward, because stillness has brought it'.[63] Only with the 'hesitating

112

step back' of pausing can the 'stillness' be heard which shuts itself off to the linear progress of the labour process. Only the 'step back' announces *walking-as-such*. Again and again, Heidegger returns to this contemplative *epoché* (stopping): "To while" [*Weilen*] means: "to tarry," "to remain still," "to pause and keep to oneself," namely in rest. In a beautiful verse Goethe says: "The fiddle stops and the dancer whiles."[64] At the very moment when the dancer stops in his movement, he becomes aware of the totality of space. This moment of hesitation is the condition for the beginning of an altogether different dance.

Gentle [*schonend*] is that 'hand resting' which refrains from violent capturing. The word '*schonen*' is derived from Middle High German '*schône*', which also means 'friendly'. Contemplative lingering is also a practice of friendliness. It lets happen, come to pass, and agrees instead of intervening. Active life without any contemplative dimension is incapable of friendly gentleness. It finds expression in accelerated production and destruction. It *uses up* time. Even in the time of leisure, which is still subject to the compulsion to labour, the relationship with time is no different. Things are destroyed and time is killed. Contemplative lingering *gives* time. It widens that being that is more than being-active. When life regains its capacity for contemplation, it gains in time and space, in duration and vastness.

If all contemplative elements are driven out of life, it ends in a deadly hyper-activity. The human being suffocates among its *own* doings. What is necessary is a revitalization of the *vita contemplativa*, because it opens up spaces for breathing. Perhaps the mind itself owes its emergence to an excess of time, an *otium*, even to a slowness of breath. A reinterpretation of *pneuma*, which means breath as well as spirit, is conceivable. Whoever runs out of breath is without spirit. The democratization of work must be followed

113

by a democratization of *otium*, lest the former turn into the bondage of everyone. Thus, Nietzsche writes:

> From lack of rest, our civilization is ending in a new barbarism. Never have the active, which is to say the restless, people been prized more. Therefore, one of the necessary correctives that must be applied to the character of humanity is a massive strengthening of the contemplative element.[65]

NOTES

Preface

1 Transl. note: '*Nichts* verhält *die Zeit.*' – This unusual form of expression is an allusion to Heidegger's use of 'comportment'.

Chapter 1 Non-Time

1 Transl. note: 'Non-time' translates '*Un-Zeit*', a neologism derived from '*Unzeit*', which is usually not used on its own but in expressions such as '*zur Unzeit*', meaning 'at an inopportune moment', or as an adjective '*unzeitgemäß*', meaning anachronistic or outmoded. The hyphenization, however, puts the stress on the prefix. As in analogously formed nouns – *Unglück* (misfortune, accident), *Unwetter* (bad weather), *Unhold* (fiend, or 'non-friend') – the prefix expresses a negation that turns something positive or neutral into something negative. In the body of the text, Han uses the word in its conventional form without hyphenization, but this translation retains the hyphenization. 'Non-time' and its derivatives, as used here, do not refer so much to an inopportune moment,

or an anachronism, but to a particular modality of time itself.

2 Friedrich Hölderlin, 'Bread and Wine', in *Selected Poems and Fragments*, trans. Michael Hamburger (London: Penguin, 1998), p. 151.

3 Nietzsche's expression *'der letzte Mensch'* is variably translated as 'the ultimate man', 'the last man' and 'the last human being'. We follow the translation of Reg Hollingdale.

4 Friedrich Nietzsche, *Thus Spoke Zarathustra*, trans. Reg Hollingdale (London: Penguin, 1961), p. 47.

5 Ibid., p. 46.

6 Ibid.

7 Nietzsche, *Zarathustra*, p. 97.

8 Ibid.

9 Ibid.

10 'Only by the anticipation of death is every accidental and "provisional" possibility driven out. Only Being-free *for* death, gives Dasein its goal outright and pushes existence into its finitude. Once one has grasped the finitude of one's existence, it snatches one back from the endless multiplicity of possibilities which offer themselves as closest to one – those of comfortableness, shirking, and taking things lightly – and brings Dasein into the simplicity of its *fate [Schicksal]*.' Martin Heidegger, *Being and Time*, trans. John Macquarrie and Edward Robinson (Oxford: Blackwell, 1973), p. 435.

11 Nietzsche, *Zarathustra*, p. 97.

12 See Heidegger, *Being and Time*, p. 164: 'In utilizing public means of transport and in making use of information services such as the newspaper, every Other is like the next. . . . We take pleasure and enjoy ourselves as *they* [man] take pleasure; we read, see, and judge about literature and art as *they* see and judge.'

13 Nietzsche, *Zarathustra*, p. 46.

14 Heidegger, *Being and Time*, p. 435.

15 Ibid., p. 438.

16 Ibid., p. 444.

17 Hartmut Rosa's monograph on *Social Acceleration: A New Theory of Modernity*, trans. Jonathan Trejo-Mathys (New York and Chichester: Columbia University Press, 2013) follows this simple line of argument.

18 Transl. note: *'Fortriß der Zeit'*: *'Riß'* ('rift') is an allusion to Heidegger's 'The Origin of the Work of Art', in which he discusses the polysemy of *'Riß'*, which may mean a rift or tear, but is also related to drawing, sketching and framing, as in *'Aufriß'* (sketch), *'Umriß'* (silhouette), or figuratively in *'Abriß'* (outline). *'Fortriß'* suggests the detachment of time from any form. See Martin Heidegger, 'The Origin of the Work of Art', in *Off the Beaten Track*, trans. Julian Young and Kenneth Haynes (Cambridge: Cambridge University Press, 2002), pp. 1–56; here p. 38 and p. 54.

19 Theodor W. Adorno, *Minima Moralia*, trans. E. N. Jephcott (London: Verso, 2005), p. 165.

20 Marcel Proust, 'Swanns Way', *In Search of Lost Time*, vol. 1, trans. C. K. Scott Moncrieff and Terence Kilmartin; revsd by D. J. Enright (London: Vintage, 1996), p. 3.

21 Ibid., p. 8.

22 Transl. note: The German translation has *'Nichts'* (nothing) in the place of 'non-being'.

23 Proust, 'Swanns Way', p. 4.

24 Ibid., p. 2.

25 Rosa, *Social Acceleration*, pp. 310f.

Chapter 2 Time without a Scent

1 Friedrich Hölderlin, 'Patmos', in *Selected Poems and Fragments*, trans. Michael Hamburger (London: Penguin, 1998), p. 239.

2 Trans. note: *'Die Zeit richtet es.'* Han plays on a double meaning of *Richten: 'to align', 'to adjust'*, and *'to judge'*.

3 Trans. note: *'nicht wiederholend, sondern einholend'*. *'Wiederholen'*

may mean 'to bring, or fetch, back' or 'to repeat'; *'einholen'* may mean 'to gather or collect' or 'to catch up with'.

4 See Reinhart Koselleck, *Futures Past: On the Semantics of Historical Time*, trans. Keith Tribe (New York/Chichester: Columbia University Press, 2004), p. 46: 'In the same way that the stars run their circular course independent of earthly men, while at the same time influencing or even determining their lives, this dual meaning resonated through the political concept of revolution from the seventeenth century on: revolutions do take place above the heads of their participants, but those concerned . . . remain imprisoned in their laws.'

5 Maximilien Robespierre, *Œuvres completes*, ed. M. Bouloiseau (Paris: Presses Universitaires de France, 1958), vol. IX, p. 495.

6 *Conversations-Lexikon der Gegenwart* (Leipzig: Brockhaus, 1838), entry on 'railways', vol. 1, p. 1136.

7 *Œuvres de Robespierre*, ed. A. Vermorel (Paris: F. Cournol, 1866), p. 276. Han quotes from Reinhard Koselleck: *Zeitschichten: Studien zur Hermeneutik* (Frankfurt/M.: Suhrkamp, 2000), p. 192.

8 Georg Büchner, *Danton's Death*, in *Complete Plays, Lenz and Other Writings*, trans. John Reddick (London: Penguin, 1993), pp. 1–73; here pp. 67–8.

9 Jean Baudrillard, 'The Millenium or The Suspense of the Year 2000', in *The Jean Baudrillard Reader*, ed. Steve Redhead (New York/Chichester: Columbia University Press, 2008), pp. 153–79; here p. 128: 'We shall never get back to pre-stereo music . . . we shall never get back to pre-news and pre-media history. The original essence of music, the original concept of history have disappeared because we shall never again be able to isolate them from their model of perfection . . . We shall never again be able to know what history was before its exacerbation into the technical perfection of news.' [Trans. note: the German translation of Baudrillard quoted by Han has 'information' instead of 'news'.]

Chapter 3 The Speed of History

1 'His life would be an uninterrupted sequence of sensations with nothing to connect them.' Denis Diderot, 'Le rêve de d'Alembert', in *Oeuvres completes*, vol. XVII, Idées IV, ed. Jean Varloot, Michel Delon, Georges Dulac and Jean Mayer (Paris: Hermann, 1984), pp. 99–100.

2 Jean Baudrillard, *The Illusion of the End*, trans. Chris Turner (Cambridge: Polity, 1994), p. 1.

3 Ibid., p. 2.

4 Ibid.

5 Ibid., pp. 3f.

6 Hartmut Rosa, *Social Acceleration: A New Theory of Modernity*, trans. Jonathan Trejo-Mathys (New York/Chichester: Columbia University Press, 2013), p. 15.

7 Ibid., p. 89.

8 Ibid., p. 314.

9 See ibid., p. 45: 'Experiences of standing still go along with the feeling of a heightening rate of change and action and even seem to be its complement or flip side.'

10 Ibid., pp. 39f.

11 Cf. Jochen Mecke, *Roman-Zeit: Zeitformen und Dekonstruktion des französischen Romans der Gegenwart* (Tübingen: Narr, 1990).

12 Michel Butor, *Passing Time*, trans. Jean Stewart (London: Simon & Schuster, 1960), p. 267.

Chapter 4 From the Age of Marching to the Age of Whizzing

1 Friedrich Nietzsche, *Thus Spoke Zarathustra*, trans. Reg Hollingdale (London: Penguin, 1961), p. 210.

2 Zygmunt Bauman, *Life in Fragments: Essays in Postmodern Morality* (Oxford: Blackwell, 1995), p. 86.

3 Ibid., p. 87.

4 *Conversations-Lexikon der Gegenwart* (Leipzig: Brockhaus, 1838), entry on 'railways', vol. 1, p. 1136.

5 Bauman, *Life in Fragments*, p. 93.
6 Hartmut Rosa, *Social Acceleration: A New Theory of Modernity*, trans. Jonathan Trejo-Mathys (New York/Chichester: Columbia University Press, 2013), p. 93.
7 Ibid., p. 207.
8 Ibid., p. 134.

Chapter 5 The Paradox of the Present

1 Maurice Blanchot, *Awaiting Oblivion*, trans. John Gregg (Lincoln: University of Nebraska Press, 1999), p. 83.
2 Transl. note: '. . . , *kann womöglich den Anschluß verpassen*'. The expression literally means 'to miss a connecting train or flight etc.', but is used metaphorically for 'losing touch with the general development of things', or 'falling behind some technical or cultural development'.

Chapter 6 Fragrant Crystal of Time

1 Marcel Proust, *In Search of Lost Time*, vol. 6, 'Time Regained', trans. C. K. Scott Moncrieff and Terence Kilmartin; revsd by D. J. Enright (London: Vintage, 2000), p. 238.
2 Ibid.
3 Ibid., vol. 5, 'The Captive'/'The Fugitive', p. 559.
4 Transl. note: '*jede Beständigkeit, ja jede Ständigkeit*' – the formulation plays on associations with 'Stand' and '*einen (festen) Stand haben*' = to have a firm hold or stand.
5 Proust, *In Search of Lost Time*, vol. 5, 'The Captive'/'The Fugitive', p. 737.
6 The sense of taste necessarily implies smells and scents. The taste of tea, in particular, consists mainly of its scent. The sensation of smells which emanate from the palate is especially intense because of the spatial closeness between the source and sense of smell.
7 Proust, *In Search of Lost Time*, vol. 1, 'Swann's Way', p. 51.

8   Ibid., vol. 6, 'Time Regained', p. 224.

9   Proust explains the feeling of happiness which runs through him as follows: 'And this cause I began to divine as I compared these diverse happy impressions, diverse yet with this in common, that I experienced them at the present moment and at the same time in the context of a distant moment, so that the past was made to encroach upon the present and I was made to doubt whether I was in the one or the other.' Ibid., p. 222.

10 Ibid., vol. 1, 'Swann's Way', p. 103. [Transl. note: The French original runs: 'vous m'évoquez encore cette vie . . . et vous la contenez en effet pour l'avoir peu à peu contournée et enclose . . . dans le cristal successif, . . ., de vos heures silencieuses, sonores, odorant et limpides'. The English translation does not retain the noun 'crystal'. *Du coté de chez Swann* (Elibron, 2007), p. 92.]

11 Ibid., vol. 6, 'Time Regained', p. 221.

12 Ibid., p. 245.

13 Ibid., p. 224.

14 Ibid., vol. 1, 'Swann's Way', pp. 54f.

15 Ibid., p. 54.

16 Ibid.

17 See Marshal McLuhan, *Understanding Media* (London/New York: Routledge, 1964), pp. 158f.

18 Ibid., p. 159.

19 Proust, *In Search of Lost Time*, vol. 6, 'Time Regained', p. 246.

20 Ibid., p. 223.

21 Ibid., p. 428.

22 Ibid., p. 246. [Transl. note: The phrase in square brackets is omitted in the English translation.]

23 Ibid., pp. 245f.

Chapter 7 The Time of the Angel

1 Rainer Maria Rilke, *Duino Elegies*, 'The First Elegy', in *Duino Elegies & Sonnets to Orpheus*, trans. Stephen Mitchell (London: Vintage, 2009), p. 2.

2 Jean François Lyotard, *The Inhuman: Reflections on Time*, trans. Geoffrey Bennington and Rachel Bowlby (Cambridge: Polity, 1991), p. 92.

3 Ibid., p. 92.

4 Ibid., p. 78.

5 Ibid., p. 87.

6 Ibid., p. 86.

7 Jean François Lyotard, *Postmodern Fables*, trans. Georges van den Abbeele (Minneapolis/London: University of Minnesota Press, 1997), p. 243.

8 Ibid., pp. 242f.

9 Ibid., p. 244.

10 Ibid., p. 245.

11 Lyotard, *The Inhuman*, p. 87.

12 Ibid., p. 92.

Chapter 8 Fragrant Clock: A Short Excursus on Ancient China

1 *Ruyi* literally means 'all as you wish'. It is a richly adorned sceptre made of wood, jade or ivory, which is supposed to bring its owner happiness, longevity and prosperity. But it can also mean 'backscratcher'.

2 Quoted after François Jullien, *Über das Fade – Ein Eloge*, trans. Andreas Hiepko and Joachim Kurtz (Berlin: Merve, 1999), p. 81. [Transl. note: The translation in the English edition of Jullien's book deviates from the German text, which is translated here. It runs: 'The flowers in the vase emerge – red,/ Incense smoke rises in pearl-grey curls,/Neither a question nor an answer,/the Ruyi lay obliquely on the ground,/Dian allowed the sound of his zither to fade away,/Zhao refrained from playing his zither:/In all this there is a melody – /

That can be sung, and can be danced.' *In Praise of Blandness: Proceeding from Chinese Thought and Aesthetics*, trans. Paula M. Varsano (New York: Zone Books, 2004), p. 76.]

3 Only the detailed documentation of Silvio A. Bedini (Curator, Division of Mechanical and Civil Engineering) drew the attention of the West to this Far Eastern practice of measuring time. See Silvio A. Bedini, 'The Scent of Time: A Study of the Use of Fire and Incense for Time Measurement in Oriental Countries', in *Transactions of The American Philosophical Society* 53/5 (1963): 1–51. Apparently, McLuhan was also familiar with this well-researched study. See Marshall McLuhan, *Understanding Media: The Extensions of Man* (London: Routledge, 1964), ch. 15: 'Clocks: The Scent of Time', pp. 157–69.

4 Quoted in Silvio A. Bedini, *The Trail of Time: Time Measurement with Incense in East Asia* (Cambridge: Cambridge University Press, 1994), p. 103.

5 *Kŏan* is the name of the succinctly formulated, often mysterious, saying which a Zen master gives to his pupils as a form of spiritual exercise.

6 See Bedini, *Trail of Time*, figure 108 (the illustrations can be found between pp. 255 and 325). [In English in the original.]

7 Ibid., figure 69. [In English in the original.]

8 Quoted in ibid., p. 130. [In English in the original.]

9 Quoted in ibid., p. 121. [In English in the original.]

10 Quoted in ibid., p. 136. [In English in the original.]

11 Quoted in ibid., p. 137. [In English in the original.]

12 Zenkei Shibayama, *The Gateless Barrier: Zen Comments on the Mumonkan* (Boston/London: Shambala, 2000), p. 146. [Transl. note: The two last lines of the German translation quoted, and subsequently referred to, by Han deviate from the English version: 'If nothing useless attaches to the human mind/This, indeed, is a good time for a human being.']

Chapter 9 The Round Dance of the World

1 Transl. note: The German text has '*Zerstörung der alltäglichen Welt*', whereas *Sein und Zeit* (Tübingen: Niemeyer, 2001), p. 105, has '*Zerstörung der alltäglichen Umwelt*', i.e. 'environment' rather than 'world'. The English translation opts for 'everyday surrounding world'. The difference between '*Welt*' and '*Umwelt*' is relevant in light of Heidegger's presentation of the animal's poverty in world, and his references to Uexküll's notion of '*Umwelt*', in *The Fundamental Concepts of Metaphysics*, trans. William McNeill and Nicholas Walker (Bloomington/Indiana: Indiana University Press, 1995), where this serves the purpose of distinguishing animals and human beings. Animals are suspended in an environment, while man is world-forming and has a world.

2 Martin Heidegger, *Being and Time*, trans. Joan Stambaugh; revised by Dennis J. Schmidt (Albany, NY: SUNY Press, 2010), pp. 102f.

3 Martin Heidegger, *On the Way to Language*, trans. Peter D. Hertz (New York: Harper & Row, 1971), p. 66.

4 Martin Heidegger, *Elucidations of Hölderlin's Poetry*, trans. Keith Hoeller (New York: Humanity Books, 2000), p. 43.

5 Heidegger, *Being and Time*, p. 331.

6 Ibid.

7 Martin Heidegger, *The Fundamental Concepts of Metaphysics: World, Finitude, Solitude*, transl. by William McNeill and Nicholas Walker (Bloomington/Indiana: Indiana University Press, 1995), p. 77.

8 Martin Heidegger, *Contributions to Philosophy (From Enowning)*, transl. by Parvis Emad and Kenneth Maly (Bloomington/Indiana: Indiana University Press, 1999), pp. 84f. [Transl. note: 'Acceleration' translates Heidegger's '*Schnelligkeit*' (speed, rapidity), see *Beiträge zur Philosophie (Vom Ereignis) (1936–1938)* (Frankfurt/ M.: Klostermann, 1989), p. 121.]

9 Heidegger, *Fundamental Concepts*, p. 129.

10 Ibid., p. 130.

11 Heidegger, *Being and Time*, pp. 372: 'Awaiting the next new thing, it [i.e. the 'they'] has already forgotten what is old. . . . Inauthentic historical existence, on the other hand, is burdened with the legacy of a 'past' that has become unrecognizable to it, looks for what is modern.'

12 Ibid., p. 370.

13 Ibid., p. 372.

14 Ibid., p. 371.

15 Ibid.

16 Ibid., p. 391. [Transl. note: The passage runs: 'Existence defined by the Moment [*augenblickliche Existenz*] temporalizes itself as fatefully whole, stretching along in the sense of the authentic, historical *constancy* of the self.' The German reads: 'Die augenblickliche Existenz zeitigt sich als schicksalhaft ganze Erstrecktheit im Sinne der eigentlichen, geschichtlichen *Ständigkeit* des Selbst.' (*Sein und Zeit*, Tübingen: Niemeyer, 2001), p. 410, i.e. it is the stretching that is fatefully whole.]

17 Ibid.

18 Ibid.

19 Martin Heidegger, 'The Pathway', trans. Thomas F. O'Meara (revisions: Thomas J. Sheehan), in *Listening. Journal of Religion and Culture* 8 (1973): 32–9; here: p. 37 (emphasis restored). Available at: <http://religious studies.stanford.edu/WWW/Sheehan/pdf/heidegger_tex ts_online/1969%20%20THE%20PATHWAY%20(Ger man%20-%20English).pdf>.

20 Martin Heidegger, *Country Path Conversations*, transl. Bret W. Davies (Bloomington/Indiana: Indiana University Press, 2010), p. 2.

21 Transl. note: The German is 'hin und her' which suggests spatial or temporal movement. The English translation has 'here and there'.

22 Martin Heidegger, *Gedachtes/Thoughts*, transl. Keith Hoeller, in *Philosophy Today* 20/4 (1976): 286–90; here p. 287. 'Wie weit?/Erst wenn sie steht, die Uhr,/im Pendelschlag des Hin und Her,/hörst Du: sie geht und ging und geht/nicht mehr./ Schon spät am Tag die Uhr,/nur blasse Spur zur Zeit,/die, nah der Endlichkeit,/aus ihr ent-steht.'

23 Heidegger, 'The Pathway', p. 33 and p. 37.

24 Ibid., p. 35 (emphases added by B-C. H.).

25 Ibid.

26 Ibid.

27 Martin Heidegger, 'The Thing', in *Poetry, Language, Thought*, trans. Albert Hofstadter (New York: HarperCollins, 2001), pp. 163–84; here: p. 178.

28 Ibid. [Transl. note: The context is Heidegger's discussion of the fourfold of earth, sky, divinities and mortals.]

29 Martin Heidegger, 'Building Dwelling Thinking', in ibid., pp. 141–59; here p. 147.

30 See ibid., p. 148.

31 Martin Heidegger, *The Thinker as Poet (Aus der Erfahrung des Denkens)*, in ibid., pp. 1–14; here p. 14. 'Wälder lagern/ Bäche stürzen/Felsen dauern/Regen rinnt. // Fluren warten/ Brunnen quellen/Winde wohnen/Segen sinnt.'

Chapter 10 The Scent of Oak Wood

1 Martin Heidegger, 'The Pathway', trans. Thomas F. O'Meara (revisions: Thomas J. Sheehan), in *Listening. Journal of Religion and Culture* 8 (1973): 32–9; here p. 35. Available at: <http://religiousstudies.stanford.edu/ WWW/Sheehan/pdf/heidegger_texts_online/1969%20 %20THE%20PATHWAY%20(German%20-%20Engl ish).pdf>.

2 Martin Heidegger, *Aus der Erfahrung des Denkens*, Gesamtausgabe, vol. 13 (Frankfurt/M.: Vittorio Klostermann, 1995), p. 153.

3 Martin Heidegger, 'The Thing', in *Poetry, Language, Thought*, trans. Albert Hofstadter (New York: HarperCollins, 2001), pp. 161–84; here p. 175.

4 Martin Heidegger, 'Building Dwelling Thinking', in ibid., pp. 141–59; here p. 147.

5 Ibid.

6 Heidegger, 'The Pathway', p. 35 [transl. mod.].

7 It is problematic that Heidegger's thought is dependent on chosen examples or on linguistic particularities such as rhyme, pronounciation or etymology. If one enters his thought at that level, it reveals itself as especially fragile, and hence vulnerable to being deconstructed. Not least because of its linguistic properties, the example of a 'jug' [*Krug*] is substantially better suited to illustrate the theory, or theology, of the thing than for instance a pitcher [*Kanne*]. Already at the level of pronunciation, the word 'jug' [*Krug*] (closing with a consonant, and having a closed vowel in the middle) displays a closedness which the word 'pitcher' [*Kanne*] lacks (where we have an open vowel and, most importantly, a further vowel at the end). Because of its closedness, the word 'jug' [*Krug*] actually holds its breath. And in addition the etymology of '*Kanne*' [from the Latin '*canna*', i.e. channel] does not suggest hold, as opposed to '*Krug*'. Rather, the word points towards flowing and flowing away. '*Krug*' is effective not only at the level of the word, but also at that of form, as it is an object that often becomes narrower towards the top, and is more closed than a '*Kanne*'. And expressions such as '*volle Kanne*' also make the word entirely unsuited to illustrate contemplative rest and calmness, which are essential to Heidegger's later philosophy. [Transl. note: '*volle Kanne*', literally 'full pitcher', is a colloquial expression for 'with full speed', or 'with the utmost intensity'.]

8 Ibid., p. 149.

9 Martin Heidegger, 'Letter on "Humanism" (1946)', trans.

Frank A. Capuzzi, in *Pathmarks* (Cambridge: Cambridge University Press. 1998), pp. 239–76; here p. 274.

10 Heidegger, 'The Pathway', p. 37.
11 Heidegger, 'The Thing', p. 179. [Transl. note: '*be-dingt*'. The verb '*bedingen*' means 'to cause' or 'to condition'.]
12 An article in *Die Zeit* which appeared after Heidegger's lecture 'On the Thing' in Munich (15 June 1950) reports: 'Behind Heidegger, a large Romanic crucifix hung on the wall. Due to the perspective it so happened that to most in the hall Heidegger appeared to be standing at Christ's feet.'
13 Martin Heidegger, *The Principle of Reason*, trans. Reginald Lilly (Bloomington/Indiana: Indiana University Press, 1991), p. 127.
14 Heidegger, 'The Pathway', pp. 37f.
15 Despite all their differences, Levinas's metaphysics of the other is based on the same temporal practice which characterizes Heidegger's thought, as he refers to exactly the same temporal figures: 'The passive synthesis of time, of patience, is a waiting without an awaited term, and one that the determinate waitings deceive, filled as they are by that which corresponds to a grasp and a *comprehension*. Time as an awaiting – as patience, more passive than any passivity correlative of acts – awaits the ungraspable.' Emmanuel Levinas, *Of God Who Comes to Mind*, trans. Bettina Bergo (Stanford/California: Stanford University Press, 1998), p. 50. In temporal terms, this ungraspable as the *Other* which evades all appropriation, any presencing [*Ver-Gegenwärtigung*], is located in the future: 'The future is what is not grasped, what befalls us and lays hold of us. The other is the future.' Emmanuel Levinas, *Time and the Other*, trans. Richard A. Cohen (Pittsburgh/PA: Duquesne University Press, 1987), p. 77.
16 Martin Heidegger, *What is Called Thinking?*, trans. J. Glenn Gray (New York: Harper & Row, 1968), p. 9.
17 Ibid., p. 17.

18 Martin Heidegger, *Contributions to Philosophy (From Enowning)*, trans. Parvis Emad and Kenneth Maly (Bloomington/Indiana: Indiana University Press, 1999), p. 277.

19 Martin Heidegger, *Elucidations of Hölderlin's Poetry*, trans. Keith Hoeller (New York: Humanity Books, 2000), p. 153.

20 Martin Heidegger, 'Postscript to "What is Metaphysics?" (1943)', trans. William McNeill, in *Pathmarks*, pp. 231–8; here p. 237.

21 Heidegger, 'The Pathway', pp. 35/37.

22 Ibid., p. 39.

23 [Transl. note: Heidegger's German text has '*lange Herkunft*', translated as 'long origin'. However, I follow Han's term '*Gewicht der "alten Herkunft"*'.]

24 For the later Heidegger, work acquires negative connotations. Thus, he speaks of the 'stupidity of simply working, which when done for itself promotes only what negates' [*das Nichtige*]. Heidegger, 'The Pathway', p. 37.

25 Ibid., p. 39.

26 Theodor W. Adorno, *Minima Moralia: Reflections on a Damaged Life*, § 54 'The Robbers', trans. E. F. N Jephcott (London, New York: Verso, 2005), pp. 89f.

27 Ibid., p. 90.

Chapter 11 Profound Boredom

1 Peter Handke, *Spuren der Verirrten* (Frankfurt/M.: Suhrkamp, 2006), p. 70.

2 Georg Büchner, *Danton's Death*, in *Complete Plays, Lenz and Other Writings*, trans. John Reddick (London: Penguin, 1993), p. 28.

3 Ibid., pp. 67f.

4 Martin Heidegger, *The Fundamental Concepts of Metaphysics*, trans. William McNeill and Nicholas Walker (Bloomington/Indiana: Indiana University Press, 1995), p. 69.

5 Ibid., p. 77.

6 Ibid., p. 162.

7 Ibid., p. 140. [Transl. note: the German expression '*Möglichkeiten des Tuns und Lassens*' = 'possibilities of doing or not doing' emphasizes that human behaviour is characterized by the possibility of *not* carrying out an act, as much as by the capacity to carry it out.]

8 Ibid., p. 163.

9 Ibid., p. 145.

10 Ibid., p. 140.

11 Ibid., p. 141.

12 Ibid., p. 149.

13 Ibid.

14 Ibid., p. 80.

15 Martin Heidegger, 'Ansprache zum Heimatabend', in *700 Jahre Stadt Meßkirch* (ed. by Stadt Meßkirch, Meßkirch, 1962), p. 13.

16 Martin Heidegger, *Contributions to Philosophy (From Enowning)*, trans. Parvis Emad and Kenneth Maly (Bloomington/Indiana: Indiana University Press, 1999), p. 84.

17 Ibid., p. 85.

18 Martin Heidegger, *Country Path Conversations*, trans. Bret W. Davis (Bloomington/Indiana: Indiana University Press, 2010), p. 100.

19 Martin Heidegger, 'Memorial Address', in *Discourse on Thinking*, trans. John M. Anderson and E. Hans Freund (New York: Harper & Row, 1966), pp. 43–57; here p. 55.

20 Heidegger, *Country Path Conversations*, p. 86.

21 Ibid., p. 94.

Chapter 12 Vita Contemplativa

1 *Hannah Arendt – Martin Heidegger: Letters 1925–1975*, ed. Ursula Ludz, trans. Andrew Shields (Orlando/Florida: Harcourt, 2004), p. 154.

2 See Aristotle, *Politics*, trans. Sir Ernest Barker (Oxford: Oxford University Press, 1995), 1333a.

3 See Aristotle, *Nicomachean Ethics*, trans. Roger Crisp (Cambridge: Cambridge University Press, 2000), pp. 6f. (1095b).

4 See Aristotle, *Politics*, pp. 300f. (1337b).

5 Kant also distinguishes between '*acumen* (*acumen*)', a special sensibility and subtlety of mind, and the activities of the understanding, which are concerned with the dimension of need. Acumen is not a kind of *work* that is informed by need, but 'a kind of intellectual luxury'. The mind is not exhausted by work and business. It is itself 'blooming', just like nature, which 'seems to be carrying on more of a game with its flowers but a business with fruits'. It would follow that knowledge is the useful fruit of unforced and playful thinking. Need and work alone would not produce it. Immanuel Kant, *Anthropology from a Pragmatic Point of View*, trans. Robert B. Louden (Cambridge: Cambridge University Press, 2006), pp. 95f.

6 Saint Augustine, *City of God*, trans. Henry Bettenson (London: Penguin, 1984), p. 880.

7 Thomas Aquinas, *Summa Theologica II*, 2, q. 182, a. 1, trans. Fathers of the English Dominican Province (Novantiqua, 2014), p. 427. [Transl. note: In the third part, almost the same phrase (*Vita contemplativa est simpliciter melior* . . .) is rendered as 'the contemplative life is, absolutely speaking, more perfect than the active life'. *Summa Theologica III*, q. 40, a.1, ad1 (Novantiqua, 2016), p. 516.]

8 Max Weber, *The Protestant Ethic and the Spirit of Capitalism*, trans. R. H. Tawney (Kettering/OH: Angelicopress, 2014), p. 68.

9 Ibid., n. 24, p. 166.

10 Quoted in ibid., n. 14, p. 164.

11 Ibid., p. 98.

12 Transl. note: '*Vermögen*' can also mean 'ability'.

13 Karl Marx, 'Economic and Philosophical Manuscripts (1844)', in *Early Writings*, trans. Rodney Livingstone and Gregor Benton (London: Penguin, 1992), pp. 279–400; here: p. 377.

14 Hannah Arendt, *The Human Condition* (Chicago and London: University of Chicago Press, 1958), p. 5.

15 Martin Heidegger, 'The Pathway', trans. Thomas F. O'Meara (revisions: Thomas J. Sheehan), in *Listening* 8 (1973): 32–9; here p. 37. Available at: <http://religiousstudies.stanford.edu/www/Sheehan/pdf/heidegger_texts_online/1969%20%20THE%20PATHWAY%20(German%20-%20English).pdf>.

16 Georg Simmel, 'Metaphysik der Faulheit. Ein Satyrspiel zur Tragödie der Philosophie' [The Metaphysics of Idleness. A Satyr Play on the Tragedy of Philosophy], in *Gesamtausgabe*, vol. 17 (Frankfurt/M.: Suhrkamp, 2005), pp. 392–397; here p. 392. Originally published in *Jugend* 20 (1900): 337–9.

17 Transl. note: '*Bilden*' and '*Bildung*' may mean both 'to educate'/'to form' and 'education'/'formation'.

18 G. W. F. Hegel, *The Phenomenology of Spirit*, trans. A. V. Miller (Oxford: Oxford University Press, 1977), p. 10.

19 Alexandre Kojève, *Introduction to the Reading of Hegel*, trans. James H. Nichols, Jr. (Ithaca, NY: Cornell University Press, 1980), p. 53.

20 Ibid., p. 43.

21 Marx, 'Economic and Philosophical Manuscripts', p. 386.

22 Simmel, 'Metaphysik der Faulheit', p. 397.

23 Karl Marx, *Grundrisse*, transl. Martin Nicolaus (London: Penguin, 1973), p. 712.

24 Thus, in *The German Ideology* it says: 'The first *historical* act of these beings, by which they differ from animals, is not that they think, but that they begin *to produce their means of subsistence.*' Karl Marx, Friedrich Engels, *Die deutsche Ideologie*, MEW 3 (Berlin: Dietz, 1969), p. 20 (emphasis restored). [Transl. note: This sentence was crossed out in Marx's origi-

nal manuscript, and is given as a footnote in the German edition, while the English edition omits it. The footnote in the German edition follows: 'The first premise of all human history is, of course, the existence of living human individuals' (*The German Ideology*, London: Lawrence & Wishart, 1970, p. 42). A few lines further down, the text makes a point that is similar, though not identical, with the one contained in the deleted sentence: 'Man can be distinguished from animals by consciousness, by religion, or by anything else you like. They themselves begin to distinguish themselves from animals as soon as they begin to produce their means of subsistence, a step that is conditioned by their physical organisation.' (ibid.)]

25 Arendt, *The Human Condition*, p. 105.

26 Friedrich Nietzsche, *The Gay Science*, trans. Josefine Nauckhoff (Cambridge: Cambridge University Press, 2001), p. 36.

27 Arendt, *The Human Condition*, p. 17. Apparently, it escaped Arendt's notice that Nietzsche was also a genius of contemplation.

28 Arendt, *The Human Condition*, p. 15.

29 Ibid.

30 Aquinas, *Summa Theologica*, II.2, q. 180, a. 6, p. 411.

31 Arendt, *The Human Condition*, p. 247.

32 Arendt, *The Human Condition*, p. 246. [Transl. note: The grammatical subject in Arendt's text is 'the faculty of action' which interrupts 'the law of mortality'. The context is her notion of 'natality' (p. 247).]

33 Ibid.

34 Thus, Nietzsche is of the opinion that the man of action, in particular, lacks *vis creativa*. In one of his aphorisms he writes: 'As the poet, he (i.e. the higher human being) certainly possesses *vis contemplativa* and a retrospective view on his work; but at the same time and above all *vis creative*, which the man of action lacks, whatever appearances and universal belief may say.' *The Gay Science*, p. 171.

35 Arendt, *The Human Condition*, p. 322.

36 Ibid.

37 Friedrich Nietzsche, *Human, All Too Human*, trans. Marion Faber (London: Faber, 1994), p. 171.

38 Arendt, *The Human Condition*, p. 321.

39 Martin Heidegger, 'The Nature of Language', in *On the Way to Language*, trans. Peter D. Hertz (New York: Harper & Row, 1971), pp. 57–108; here p. 57.

40 Arendt, *The Human Condition*, p. 242.

41 Ibid., p. 246.

42 Transl. note: This is a reference to a collection of poems by Paul Celan: *Breathturn*, trans. Pierre Joris (Los Angeles: Green Integer, 2006).

43 Ibid., p. 325. [Transl. note: The German edition deviates from the English and does not contain the phrase 'power of acting individuals'.]

44 Aristotle, *Nicomachean Ethics*, p. 195 (1178b). [Transl. note: The German translation has 'the possibility of action based on ethical virtue and wisdom'.]

45 Arendt, *The Human Condition*, p. 325. [Transl. note: According to the English translation of Cicero, Cato relates a remark actually made by Africanus: 'Such a man, finally, can say of himself the same thing Cato writes that my grandfather Africanus used to say, that he never did more than when he did nothing, that he was never less alone than when he was alone.' Cicero, *On the Commonwealth and On the Laws* (Cambridge: Cambridge University Press, 1999), p. 13.]

46 Cicero, *On the Commonwealth and On the Laws*, p. 14.

47 Friedrich Nietzsche, *Thus Spoke Zarathustra*, trans. Reg Hollingdale (London: Penguin, 1969), p. 73.

48 See Arendt, *The Human Condition*, p. 324. [Transl. note: The passage runs: 'As a living experience, thought has always been assumed, perhaps wrongly, to be known only to the few. It

may not be presumptuous to believe that these few have not become fewer in our time.']

49 Nietzsche, *Human, All Too Human*, p. 170.

50 Ibid., p. 171.

51 Immanuel Kant, *Anthropology from a Pragmatic Point of View*, trans. Robert B. Louden (Cambridge: Cambridge University Press, 2006), p. 96.

52 Nietzsche, *The Gay Science*, p. 184.

53 Martin Heidegger, 'Science and Reflection', in: *The Question Concerning Technology and Other Essays*, trans. William Lovitt (New York: Harper & Row, 1977), pp. 155–82; here p. 166.

54 As so often, Heidegger fabricates this *argumentative* transition by way of a linguistic–etymological hint: 'The German translation for *contemplatio* is Betrachtung [view or observation].' (ibid.)

55 Ibid., p. 167.

56 Aquinas, *Summa Theologica II*, q. 180, a. 4, p. 400.

57 Quoted in Alois M. Haas, 'Die Beurteilung der Vita contemplativa and activa in der Dominikanermystik des 14. Jahrhunderts', in *Arbeit Musse Meditation*, ed. B. Vickers (Zürich, 1985), pp. 109–31; here p. 113.

58 Heidegger, 'The Pathway', p. 35 (transl. mod.).

59 Heidegger, 'Science and Reflection', p. 181.

60 'The word *bilden* [to form or cultivate] means first: to set up a preformed model [*Vor-bild*] and to set forth a preestablished rule [*Vor-schrift*]. It means, further, to give form to inherent tendencies. Intellectual cultivation brings before man a model in the light of which he shapes and improves all that he does. ... As over against this, reflection first brings us onto the way toward the place of our sojourning.' (Heidegger, 'Science and Reflection', pp. 180f.)
'Through reflection so understood we actually arrive at the place where, without having experienced it and without having seen penetratingly into it, we have long been sojourning.

135

In reflection we gain access to a place from out of which there first opens the space traversed at any given time by all our doing and leaving undone.' (Heidegger, 'Science and Reflection', p. 180.)

61 Martin Heidegger, 'Science and Reflection', ibid.
62 Martin Heidegger, 'A Dialogue on Language', in *On the Way to Language*, pp. 1–56; here p. 16.
63 Ibid. – Cf. Martin Heidegger, 'Remembrance': 'Its hesitation [i.e. that of shyness] is the expectant decisiveness to be patient. Here, hesitation is the courage to go slowly, a courage decided long ago. The hesitation of shyness is forbearance.' In *Elucidations of Hölderlin's Poetry*, trans. Keith Hoeller (New York: Humanity Books, 2000), pp. 101–74; here p. 153.
64 Martin Heidegger, *The Principle of Reason*, trans. Reginald Lilly (Bloomington/Indiana: Indiana University Press, 1991), p. 127.
65 Nietzsche, *Human, All Too Human*, p. 172.